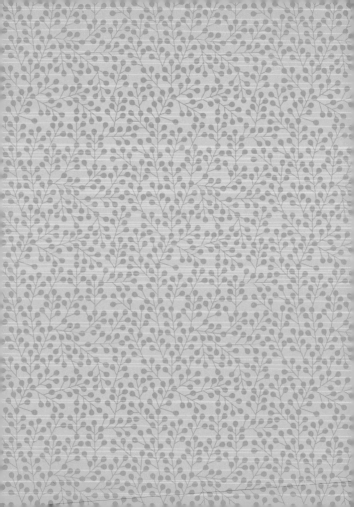

To:

From:

Message:

One-Minute Devotions® for Young Women

© 2015 Christian Art Gifts, RSA
        Christian Art Gifts Inc., IL, USA

First edition 2015

Cover designed by Christian Art Gifts

Images used under license from Shutterstock.com

Unless otherwise indicated, all Scripture quotations are taken from the *Holy Bible*, New Living Translation®. Copyright © 1996, 2004, 2007 by Tyndale House Publishers, Inc., Carol Stream, Illinois 60188. All rights reserved.

Printed in China

ISBN 978-1-4321-1235-6

18 19 20 21 22 23 24 25 26 27 – 15 14 13 12 11 10 9 8 7 6

ONE-MINUTE DEVOTIONS®

for YOUNG
WOMEN

Mallory Larsen

christian
art gifts®

January

STRENGTH IN WEAKNESS

*Moses pleaded with the L*ORD*, "O Lord, I'm not very good with words. I never have been, and I'm not now, even though You have spoken to me. I get tongue-tied, and my words get tangled." Then the L*ORD *asked Moses, "Who makes a person's mouth? Who decides whether people speak or do not speak, hear or do not hear, see or do not see? Is it not I, the L*ORD*? Now go! I will be with you as you speak, and I will instruct you in what to say."*

EXODUS 4:10-12

It can be easy to focus on our weaknesses. Often-times, they feel glaringly obvious and leave us feeling extremely inept. Hopelessness may feel like the only option when faced with our own inabilities. What do you do with the areas in your life that leave you feeling unskilled? Do you let them define you or do you trust that you are not alone, even in your shortcomings?

Recognizing our areas of weakness should not be a call to self-loathing, but an invitation to let God be our help and strength.

Whatever the struggle, God can give us the expertise needed to live our lives in a way that honors Him and serves others.

January 1

SPEAKING WITHOUT WORDS

When they were discouraged, I smiled at them.
My look of approval was precious to them.

JOB 29:24

Isn't it amazing how a curve of the mouth knows no language barrier? No matter where we are in the world, a smile can communicate kindness, warmth, welcoming and acceptance.

In a world littered with senseless violence, hate and darkness, a smile can be a powerful tool to bring light into our communities.

It may seem like a small act, but smiling at those we walk past on the sidewalk, see in the grocery store or stop next to at a red light actually has the power to turn a person's day around.

Why not try to share kindness with a stranger – especially since we don't even have to find the words to speak! Something as simple as a smile to a stranger could spread from her to someone else, to someone else, to someone else …

January 2

GIVE & TAKE

*All must give as they are able, according to
the blessings given to them by the LORD your God.*

DEUTERONOMY 16:17

It's hard not to stockpile our belongings. What if our money, food or clothing runs out? What if we give to those in need and then don't have enough left for ourselves?

It can be a scary feeling to admit when we are in a position to give to others. We may be left wondering if our blessings will dry out.

Here's the thing: if each of us gives as we are able, then our blessings are not simply being emptied, they are being shared. You may give to me, but someone else, then, may give to you.

Take stock of your money, food, clothing or even your joy – let's consider giving to others, trusting that the Lord will continue to bless us through others.

January 3

GETTING A GRIP!

"Don't sin by letting anger control you."
Don't let the sun go down while you are still
angry, for anger gives a foothold to the devil.

EPHESIANS 4:26-27

Anger is a powerful emotion. It can drive us to say or do things that are regrettable, hurtful and out of character.

While anger may not be completely unavoidable, it is not meant to be in command of our words and actions. Once we allow anger to rule over us in a moment or circumstance, we are handing ourselves over to sin.

What if, instead of letting anger dictate our behavior, we do something with it? A moment to pray, go for a walk, journal or have a conversation with someone we are struggling with can alter the way we behave in anger.

Even if the anger doesn't completely go away, it will no longer be in control – and neither will sinfulness!

January 4

PATIENTLY WAITING

*Each morning I bring my requests
to You and wait expectantly.*

PSALM 5:3

Do you ever ask for something without waiting to hear the answer? Maybe you know your request is a long shot, or maybe you have no doubt that the response will be a resounding "YES!" Either way, isn't it interesting that you would ask something but not pause to listen to the answer?

God wants to receive our requests and offer us a response. We might hear an immediate answer, or we could have our patience tested as we pause to listen.

God's response is worth waiting around for – ask for what you need and desire, but don't forget to stand by for His response!

A HOLY HAND-OFF

Give all your worries and cares
to God, for He cares about you.

1 PETER 5:7

It can be difficult to remain grounded in the midst of stressful or scary circumstances. Anxiety is usually an overwhelming and lonely feeling. Where do you go when life begins to feel like "too much?" Who do you talk to? Or do you keep it all to yourself?

Stressful times will come and go (and then come again), but God's care for us is not going anywhere. While we may not always be able to completely escape worries or anxiety, we are free to give them to God, rather than hold on to them ourselves.

God cares about what worries us, no matter how big or small it may seem. When we share it with Him, the load of our anxiety is lightened, and peace enters into the chaos.

January 6

EYES TO SEE, HEART TO KNOW

The LORD said to Samuel, "Don't judge by his appearance or height, for I have rejected him. The LORD doesn't see things the way you see them. People judge by outward appearance, but the LORD looks at the heart."

1 SAMUEL 16:7

What is going through your mind when you first see someone? Do you analyze their size, wonder about their outfit choice or rate their hairstyle? Do you find yourself making assumptions about who they are as a person, based on what your eyes are telling you?

It can be easy to allow our eyes to tell us about a person's character, but our eyes alone cannot know the depth of a person's heart. God does not look at our appearance to see who we are. He looks inward, at our heart.

Next time your eyes begin to jump to conclusions about someone, take some time to get to know their heart – spend time together, ask them questions and get to know them from the inside, out.

DIVINE BODYGUARDS

He will order His angels to
protect you wherever you go.

PSALM 91:11

Have you ever walked alone in the dark and found yourself looking back to ensure that no one was following you? Or maybe you've ventured into a neighborhood or city that experiences a great deal of violence.

It could be that you are facing a life circumstance that causes you fear or pain – your heart is broken, an illness arises or a financial burden is felt. Fear can be crippling, most especially when we feel alone in a dark, scary situation.

How does it change things to know that God's presence and the protection of His angels surrounds us, even when we're walking along dark streets or through dark times?

Next time you are feeling afraid, remember the presence of the unseen all around you; rest assured that you are not alone.

January 8

A PERMANENT FIX

*Truthful words stand the test
of time, but lies are soon exposed.*

PROVERBS 12:19

Have you ever told a little white lie? What about a great big lie? Was it difficult to keep track of what untruths you told, and whom you told them to? Telling lies can easily become a complicated way to live because we're required to keep track of the falsities we're speaking, so as to not be exposed in our untruths.

While it may not always be easy to tell the truth, the truth is what will remain, no matter what. Although telling a lie may be the more desirable route to take in a given moment, it is only but a temporary "fix".

Almost immediately but always eventually, lies will be stripped away to reveal the truth, which always remains.

FITTING RIGHT IN

Listen to the LORD who created you.
O Israel, the one who formed you says,
"Do not be afraid, for I have ransomed you.
I have called you by name; you are Mine."

ISAIAH 43:1

Do you ever feel like you just don't belong? Does it seem as if everyone else has a place where they fit in, and you are a wanderer, looking for somewhere to land? It's difficult to see tight-knit groups of friends together or others who have found their passions in life, while we are left feeling alone, abandoned or unseen.

It feels good to have a place where we fit in and, thanks be to God, we do! We are God's beloved creation. He calls us each by name and sees our individuality and uniqueness.

When we recognize that we belong to Him, we can stop our wandering and rest in knowing that we will always have a place as daughters of the King.

January 10

MAKE WAY FOR JOY!

*Each heart knows its own bitterness,
and no one else can fully share its joy.*

PROVERBS 14:10

Have you ever offered a half-hearted "congratulations" through gritted teeth when a friend shares news about a job promotion, engagement or exciting purchase? Though "congratulations!" is meant to express joy, it can easily be saturated with jealousy.

The bitterness we hold in our own hearts robs us of the joy we can share with others, both in their accomplishments and in our own. When bitterness begins to take up residence in our hearts, it leaves little room for joy to remain, so we are left having to choose one or the other.

Today, fight against bitterness and choose joy – notice the difference it makes in your own happiness and in your relationship with others.

BROKEN BUT NOT ALONE

The LORD is close to the brokenhearted;
He rescues those whose spirits are crushed.

PSALM 34:18

The loss of a loved one, an ended relationship, a difficult diagnosis. The paths to a broken heart are plenty, and each is wrought with pain, grief and suffering.

There is no quick-fix when it comes to a broken heart, but navigating the pain alone is immeasurably more difficult than being joined in the deep sorrow of the circumstance.

It is good to have someone who will join us in our grief. A hug, a listening ear or wise advice can aid us greatly in our pain. We also have access to God in our heartache. He is with us in the desolate moments, desiring to bring us up from the depth of our pain.

Talk to Him when you are feeling despair; let yourself be aware of His presence in your brokenness, and be encouraged by the hope of His healing power.

BETTER TOGETHER

*Share each other's burdens, and
in this way obey the law of Christ.*

GALATIANS 6:2

Imagine a friend is on a long hike to a desirable location. The pack on their back is heavy and their hands are full. If you were to come alongside them and take some items off of their hands, how would that impact the hike? The hiker would probably be able to go a lot farther in a shorter amount of time, and the journey, though still difficult, would be more manageable.

Life can be hard. No matter where you're from or what your circumstances are like, it is certain that you will not escape pain or difficulties. This is something we all have in common.

The gift of community is one that God gave us so that we may not only enjoy life together in joy, but so that we can come alongside one another in difficulties, as well.

How can you help carry the load of someone's burdens today?

POWERFUL TOOLS

*The tongue is a small thing that
makes grand speeches. But a tiny
spark can set a great forest on fire.*

JAMES 3:5

Sticks and stones may break my bones, but words will never hurt me!

This catchy expression has been tauntingly sung amongst children for decades. What few will admit, however, is that it is actually completely untrue. Sticks and stones may break a bone or bruise the skin, but words cut us deep within. Sticks and stones may leave a scar on our bodies, but hurtful words are even harder to recover from – we often carry them around with us, letting them live in the dark and painful places in our soul.

The words we speak can either be a weapon used to hurt, or a tool to bring encouragement and love into the lives of others. Words do not simply roll off the tongue and float away; they stick to the person receiving them and either cut or gladden their heart. Choose to speak words that are a tool for God rather than a weapon for evil!

January 14

Mallory Larsen

AN UNCHANGING GOD IN A REVOLVING WORLD

Jesus Christ is the same
yesterday, today, and forever.

HEBREWS 13:8

Take one look at popular fashion, music and movies throughout the decades and it's clear: things change. What was considered popular or attractive one year may be laughable a few years later. Sometimes, on a more painful level, people and relationships change, as well. Over time, we grow and transform as we are shaped by our communities and experiences. The prevalence of change all around us may be exciting or unsettling – either way, it is a reality of our existence.

We can ground ourselves, however, in the truth that God is unchanging. Although the fads of our younger days may expire or we may no longer be compatible with the best friend we once had, how reassuring it is to know that Jesus stays the same. The One we put our faith in, the relationship we cultivate with the Divine, will not transform with the passing time – what sweet security in our ever-changing world.

BIG FEARS, BIGGER GOD

The LORD is my light and my
salvation – so why should I be afraid?
The LORD is my fortress, protecting me
from danger, so why should I tremble?

PSALM 27:1

What are you afraid of? Take a minute to think about the things that scare you the most, and then wonder about what it is that is scary about those things. Whether it is a fear of flying or of the ocean, having an illness or losing a loved one – no matter the fear, is there anything scary that is bigger than God, more powerful than our Creator, or more able than our heavenly Father?

We all have fears, but they need not paralyze or control us, because our God is in control, protecting His people from that which is dark, scary and dangerous. You may not automatically love to travel by airplane or swim in the ocean, but you know you can do those things because God has already saved us from eternal death. Our fear does not get the final say, because God has already spoken, and He has claimed everlasting life for us!

January 16

WILD WONDERS

Ask the LORD your God for a sign of confirmation,
Ahaz. Make it as difficult as you want – as high
as heaven or as deep as the place of the dead.

ISAIAH 7:11

Have you ever asked a parent or a friend for something outrageous – a request that you knew would never actually be granted?

Or maybe you didn't ask because you figured it wasn't even worth speaking the question aloud. It is good to dream and desire big and wild things; and, so too, it can be scary.

While we may have an idea of which requests are too outrageous for a friend or family member to grant, God, the Maker of the Universe, is able to do extraordinary things for us and with us.

We can bring our wild requests to Him and be confident that while they may not be granted, they certainly could be!

NO SECRETS!

If we confess our sins to Him,
He is faithful and just to forgive us our sins
and to cleanse us from all wickedness.

1 JOHN 1:9

It's not fun to admit when we have messed up. Wouldn't it be nice if we could keep all of our mistakes and sins to ourselves, so no one else would have to know about them? Although that sounds wonderful, it is definitely not realistic.

The bad news is, we sin and make mistakes. The good news, though, is that when we acknowledge our sinfulness to God, admitting when we've done wrong and expressing repentance for our actions, we experience God's extravagant grace in His full forgiveness of our sins!

We, then, have the choice: hold on to the secrets of our sins, or find freedom through sharing our shortcomings with God and allow His grace to restore us.

January 18

WORTHLESS WORRIES

*"Can all your worries add
a single moment to your life?"*

LUKE 12:25

There is always plenty to worry about. Money, work, relationships, health – we could easily become overwhelmed with anxiety. What good, however, comes from worrying?

Does our worry over a particular situation ease or enhance our anxiety? Does the worrisome circumstance improve at all because of our worry? And, where is our faith in God's protection when our anxiety feels closer than His presence?

It's not always easy to give our worries to God, but it is in doing just that where we can find peace. Our stress in difficult circumstances does not change the circumstance – it only negatively impacts our well-being.

Take a deep breath, share your worries with the One who can save you and welcome peace into the chaos.

January 19

HOLY REFLECTIONS

*Fix your thoughts on what is true,
and honorable, and right, and pure,
and lovely, and admirable. Think about
things that are excellent and worthy of praise.*

PHILIPPIANS 4:8

Isn't it amazing how every aspect of our lives reflects who we are in Christ? God is not revealed in us only by how often we pray, read our Bible or attend church. God is revealed in our language, the movies we watch and the websites we visit. What we allow to fill our mind communicates what we value the most.

When the movies we watch, music we listen to, language we use and hobbies we partake in are pleasing, rather than dishonoring, to God, then our life will reflect His presence and goodness.

When God fills our thoughts, we can't help but live a life that honors Him!

January 20

YOUR GIFT – AND MINE!

*Salvation is not a reward for the good things
we have done, so none of us can boast about it.*

EPHESIANS 2:9

It's pretty cool that God has given us the gift of salvation, isn't it? I mean, that's a pretty huge gift! That's just it – it's a gift. It's not a reward for good behavior, it's a selfless offering given out of deeply authentic love to all who want to receive it.

Bragging about the hope and life we have in Jesus Christ completely goes against the values of Christ. Instead of bragging about this gift, what about sharing it with others?

Supplies are not limited here – there is enough salvation to go around and we get to be someone who tells others that a gift is waiting for them (rather than purely boasting about this gift we have received)!

January 21

WHAT'S GOOD WITH YOU?

Anger is cruel, and wrath is like a flood,
but jealousy is even more dangerous.

PROVERBS 27:4

"She has a nicer car, more clothes and a better figure." Or maybe, "He's smarter, she's more athletic, he's funnier." People around us seem to have more friends, higher-paying jobs and committed relationships. Jealousy can creep into our thoughts about others very easily and sometimes unnoticed.

Particularly in this day and age, with the rise of social media, we are being inundated with photos and snippets of what is "good" in other people's lives. Are we even aware when we're thinking a jealous thought or making a jealous remark?

Jealousy drives a wedge between us and other people – it creates bitterness in our relationships and robs us of joy and gratitude for what we have in our own lives.

This week, try to notice when jealousy is present in your thoughts or words and counter it by focusing on something you are grateful for.

January 22

INESCAPABLE LOVE

*Even if my father and mother abandon
me, the LORD will hold me close.*

PSALM 27:10

It's hard to think about a mother or father abandoning their child, but it happens – probably more than any of us would care to know. Maybe it has even happened to you. How painful that the man and woman who united to create the little one who grew inside the mother's womb, would then desert the one who shares their DNA.

Though this is unfathomable for some, and a deeply tragic reality for others, it makes it all the more outstanding that we can trust that even if our mother and father leave us, God will not only remain with us, but He will hold us close. This is a significant promise, which communicates the sincerity of God's desire to be with us.

If we feel alone because of abandonment from family or separation from loved ones, may we remember that the One who formed us in our mother's womb is not going anywhere – He will hold us close.

January 23

BEING THE LIGHT OF A DAY

Love each other with genuine affection,
and take delight in honoring each other.

ROMANS 12:10

Have you ever surprised a friend with a gift you knew they would love? Or have you taken time out of your day to serve someone who needed some help? It really does feel good to love others well, especially when we, too, are loved well.

How can you honor someone else today? Maybe you could write an encouraging note to a co-worker, buy lunch for a friend or wash your sister's car. Honoring one another does not require grand gestures (though it can!), but is done through little acts of service and kindness that reflect Christ's love.

Today, be intentional in showing affection to others – and take delight!

January 24

Mallory Larsen

STEPPING STONES

Do not despise these small beginnings,
for the LORD rejoices to see the work begin.

ZECHARIAH 4:10

"Baby steps" take patience. When a baby takes her first steps, she is wobbly and uncertain, taking one or two steps before falling over, possibly even regressing in the progress of distance spanned. However, without beginning with these slow and unsteady steps, she would never walk (or run, skip or leap!). Small beginnings, though frustrating, are exactly what is necessary to move towards greater things.

What sort of "baby steps" are you taking these days? How can you celebrate your progress, even if it is slow? Maybe today you stood up (and only stood up). Maybe tomorrow you'll take two steps and maybe the following day you will take two more. Be patient in your wobbly steps, for they are the stepping-stones to great big leaps!

January 25

UNJUST, UNFAIR, UNMOVED

The fastest runner doesn't always win the race, and the strongest warrior doesn't always win the battle. The wise sometimes go hungry, and the skillful are not necessarily wealthy.

ECCLESIASTES 9:11

It's JUST NOT FAIR!

Being faced with the injustices of life is hardly something we can ever grow accustomed to. If you're the hardest worker – the most dedicated, honest and courageous – then you deserve to be the most re-warded, recognized and honored. Right?!

Well, right! It would be a perfect world if fairness reigned in all situations. We all know, however, that this is not a perfect world. Life is not fair and no amount of work or desire can control the maddening injustices. How can we reconcile that?

In reconciling, we have a decision to make. Will we continue to live dedicated, honest, courageous lives, possibly without recognition; or will we give up, releasing our efforts and live small, defeated by the reality of our unfair world? We may not be able to control unfairness, but we can remain virtuous, even still.

January 26

MY OWN WORK

*"Why worry about a speck in your friend's
eye when you have a log in your own?"*

MATTHEW 7:3

Did you hear what she did!? Can you even believe that happened? How could she do such a thing? It's hardly believable. She's just awful!

It can sometimes feel affirming to discuss the shortcomings of another person – maybe, then, we won't feel so alone or severe in our "badness." When we're focusing on the sins of others, we don't have to recognize our own sins. God, however, calls us to more. Whatever "she" did might sound horrible, but God says that we need not worry about it, for we have our own sins to account for. There is nothing honorable about bypassing our own sin to talk about the fault of another person.

Trust that God will take care of whatever situation "she" is in, and recognize your own need for a Savior. We are not more (or less) sinful than others, and there is still work to be done in our own hearts – focus on that!

A WORTHY PAUSE

After the earthquake there was a fire,
but the LORD was not in the fire. And after
the fire there was the sound of a gentle whisper.

1 KINGS 19:12

Sometimes it feels as if the "fire," or the difficulties, in our lives will wage on forever. Where is God in the midst of the pain and destruction taking place? We may only feel the burning flames of a deeply painful and scary circumstance, without sensing His presence in the midst of the heat.

Pause. Hold on. The fire will die down and the smoke will subside and, wait – did you hear that? His still, small voice is like a shot of cool air over the burning embers.

Destruction will come into our lives in various forms, making it difficult to sense God's closeness. If you don't feel Him in the earthquake or the fire, trust that His voice is there, whispering in the aftermath, "Here I am. You are not alone."

January 28

THE DISTINCTNESS OF YOU

*In His grace, God has given us different
gifts for doing certain things well.*

ROMANS 12:6

I wish I could sing. Life would be so much easier if I were good at budgeting. She's so much better with kids than I am. You're the funny one. I'm always so disorganized.

When we focus only on the skills we lack (and others possess), it's no wonder that we become discouraged with ourselves. If you had *her* people skills, *his* intelligence, or *their* passion, *then* you would be worthy, useful and admirable.

Our Creator God is *not* boring – that is for certain. What sort of world would it be if we each had the same gifts? Seven billion talented singers, mathematicians or comedians would make for a pretty dull existence. What are you good at? Even if you only name one or two gifts of yours, embrace those. They are needed, and they help to create a world of diversity, where our gifts can serve one another.

January 29

PARTY TIME, ANY TIME!

*Go and celebrate with a feast of rich foods
and sweet drinks, and share gifts of food with
people who have nothing prepared. This is a
sacred day before our Lord. Don't be dejected
and sad, for the joy of the LORD is your strength!*

NEHEMIAH 8:10

Who doesn't love a good party? It is fun to celebrate birthdays, graduations and weddings with friends. If celebrating is so much fun, though, why wait for a special occasion? Can't the goodness we experience with good food and laughter be enough of a reason to gather together?

Knowing and living a life with God instills within us a deep-seated joy that can hardly keep us from wanting to throw a party! So, why not? Invite friends *and* people you may not know very well.

Let everyone bask in the delight of food, drink, laughter, conversation and the gladness of God's presence. God-inspired celebrations are rich with the most earnest form of joy!

January 30

RISKS WORTH TAKING!

*"Bring all the tithes into the storehouse
so there will be enough food in My Temple.
If you do," says the LORD of Heaven's Armies,
"I will open the windows of heaven for you.
I will pour out a blessing so great you won't have
enough room to take it in! Try it! Put Me to the test!"*

MALACHI 3:10

Giving away some of our money or belongings can be hard! Sure, other people need food, clothing and shelter, but what about us? Yes, the Bible says to tithe every week, but does it really mean *every* week? That's a lot of weeks! What if we tithe one week and then don't have enough money for food the following week? That's a risky move!

The thing is, God knows it is risky, because He so richly blesses those who give to others. Tithing is an act of faith, trusting that what we give to God, He will return to us (and He may even multiply our return!).

This verse is a challenge to us – commit to tithing to God's kingdom each week, and let Him show us the blessings that are in store for us!

January 31

AGING GRACEFULLY

*We grow weary in our present bodies, and we long
to put on our heavenly bodies like new clothing.*

2 Corinthians 5:2

As you get older, what sort of changes do you begin to *feel* in your body? Does your back ache, has your strength weakened and your eyeglass prescription strengthened?

As we age, we become increasingly aware that our bodies are not immortal. We grow tired, experience pain, and may even fall seriously ill. Our bodies are capable of doing incredible things, but they eventually fail us.

The promise of one day receiving our heavenly body can bring deep comfort when we're struggling in our imperfect earthly body.

The limitations of our body can be discouraging, but an upgrade is in store! Until then, we should honor this earthly casing for our soul – it's ours for the entirety of our time spent on this side of heaven!

February 1

SAFELY UNCOMFORTABLE

*"Yes, come," Jesus said. So Peter went over the side
of the boat and walked on the water toward Jesus.
But when he saw the strong wind and the waves,
he was terrified and began to sink. "Save me, Lord!"
he shouted. Jesus immediately reached out and grabbed him.*

MATTHEW 14:29-31

Have you ever felt called to do something that required you to risk something, or been asked to take on a role that demanded courage? Following God does not mean that we will remain in the safety of our comfort zone. He is a wild and untamable God, who loves when we live wildly for Him. He may call us to do the unthinkable, but He is certainly not a God who will call us to get out of the boat and then watch what happens from the shore.

God may be calling us to do outrageous, unpredictable or terrifying things, but we can be sure that He is not shouting instructions at us from a safe distance. He's one step ahead of us – He's already on the water when He calls us to get out of the boat. His hand is ready to hold ours as we follow Him in this wild life on earth!

February 2

ENOUGH IS ENOUGH!

True godliness with contentment is itself
great wealth. After all, we brought nothing
with us when we came into the world, and
we can't take anything with us when we leave it.

1 TIMOTHY 6:6-7

It's easy for most of us to accumulate a lot of stuff throughout our lives — or to spend a lot of time desiring more stuff. Clothes, jewelry, electronics, books, shoes, makeup, movies — that which is our "stuff" is a lengthy list. It takes up space in our homes and in our minds, oftentimes distracting us from what is really important.

While it is good to have some "stuff," we are being wasteful of our time and resources when we continue to accumulate more than we need. In the end, our stuff will continue to sit in our homes long after our earthly bodies meet their death. It might be time to reconsider what is so important about having all that "stuff," and consider giving some of it away to those who are in need, allowing us to refocus our attention on our relationships with people and with God, rather than with our stuff.

February 3

NOT "IF," BUT "HOW?"

"What do you mean, 'If I can'?" Jesus asked.
"Anything is possible if a person believes."

MARK 9:23

"If" is a tiny word with a big presence. With just two letters, "if" can shift a statement from being declarative to being conditional. Your boss might respond to your request regarding if it is possible for you to take a day off by saying, "Yes (Great news!); if you work late tonight (Bummer)."

When we bring our requests to God, "if" isn't such a big factor. To Him, responding to our prayers is not a matter of whether or not it is possible or He is able; the only condition is placed in whether or not we believe in God's ability to hear and respond to us.

While this doesn't mean that every prayer of ours will be answered (His will be done!), know that His ability to answer us need not be in question.

February 4

COME OUT, COME OUT, WHEREVER YOU ARE!

God has invited you into partnership
with His Son, Jesus Christ our Lord.

1 CORINTHIANS 1:9

Have you ever been persistently pursued by someone? Maybe they continually invited you to share a meal, a cup of coffee or a walk with them. They might have sent you encouraging letters or thoughtful gifts. You may have welcomed this pursuit, or maybe it grew tiresome.

Regardless, what did it feel like to be so desired? If this isn't an experience you have had, what do you imagine it would feel like to have someone seek you out so intentionally?

Well – you, dear one, are desired. You are being pursued by the God of the universe! He wants to commune with us, He wants us to share our life with Him. He is not a pushy pursuer, but He is incessant. He calls, and He waits – always desiring to spend time with you.

February 5

TEAM BUILDING

Why do you condemn another believer?
Why do you look down on another believer?

ROMANS 14:10

Imagine playing on a competitive sport team that thrives on each teammate's peak performance. What happens when one player messes up? Do her teammates blame, disgrace or even exclude her from feeling a sense of belonging on her team?

While it can be frustrating when a team member makes a mistake, particularly one that impacts the entire team, it seems senseless to punish them so severely when the team is working towards the same goals.

As human beings, it is impossible to have a team or community that is made up of perfect members. We will all mess up in one way or another, and more than once too. As members of the body of Christ, we will disappoint each other in our shortcomings. Instead of belittling one another, let's recognize the shared desires we have in following Christ, and build one another up when we fail, rather than tear each other down even more.

February 6

[THE EVENTUAL] HAPPY EVER AFTER!

He will wipe every tear from their eyes, and there will be no more death or sorrow or crying or pain.

REVELATION 21:4

Think about all of the movies that have "fairytale endings." The big problem is solved, the girl and guy get together and everyone lives happily ever after. Sounds pretty great, doesn't it? What happens, though, when we turn the movie off and get back to real life? There are dishes in the sink, bills to pay and relational conflicts to face. Where is *our* happily ever after?

Well, here's the good news: *it's coming.* Living with and for God means that we are guaranteed the *ultimate* "happily ever after!" When we leave our earthly bodies and go to heaven, we will also be leaving behind all of our pain, anxiety and struggles. Our disappointments, failures and grief will be no more, and our eternity in heaven will be filled with joy and deep fulfillment, better than any movie ending we can even imagine!

February 7

WANT VERSUS NEED

The Lord is my shepherd; I have all that I need.

PSALM 23:1

Take a look at the people and communities surrounding you. Are there more people "in want" or "in need?" What about in your own life – do your desires reflect that which you want, or that which you need?

It is not bad to want things. Our desires are meaningful and our "wants" may very well align with something God wants to bless us with. However, when we blur the lines between wants and needs, we are likely missing out on an opportunity to express gratefulness.

Let's take some time today to acknowledge our needs. Are they being met? If so, that is a cause for celebration and praising God! If not, can we share our needs with Him (and maybe with others too?)? Praise God today for how He meets our needs and honors our wants!

BEING SEEN

*Don't let anyone think less of you
because you are young. Be an example
to all believers in what you say, in the way
you live, in your love, your faith, and your purity.*

1 TIMOTHY 4:12

Who do you look up to? Whose example are you following? Do you only look to those who are older, or do you take note of the words and actions of your peers? What about a younger man or woman who is living a particularly exemplary life?

It can be easy to assume that our actions are not being seen or modeled until we are older and, assumedly, wiser. It's true that we can learn a lot from our elders, but we are never too young to set an example of what it means to live a godly life.

Regardless of how many years we've been on this earth, our life, experiences and actions hold value that those around us can see and, hopefully, learn from. May our lives reflect our faith so that others may be encouraged!

PLACES OF PEACE

*In every place of worship, I want men
to pray with holy hands lifted up to
God, free from anger and controversy.*

1 TIMOTHY 2:8

Being in community with others can be incredibly difficult, even if it is a community of believers. We are not sinless or blameless, even within our churches and Christian circles. Our places of worship, however, should be places of peace.

When we enter our Christian community, we should be able to feel a sense of rest, rather than facing controversy, anxiety or fear. This peace and harmony will, ideally, travel outside of the walls of our church into the other relationships and communities in our lives. If we can't begin with peace in our church, it will be much harder to bring God's love and peace into other places of our lives.

Let's practice peace and warm fellowship in our Christian community, and then carry it on to our other communities! Let God's love and kindness live in our churches and fill us each week, so we may share it with others!

February 10

OUR RESCUER

Say to those with fearful hearts, "Be strong,
and do not fear, for your God is coming to
destroy your enemies. He is coming to save you."

ISAIAH 35:4

Do you ever just want to be rescued? It doesn't have to be a knight in shining armor riding in on a white horse, but someone to take away our burdens or bring peace to our troubles would be nice! We can do what we can to help each other out but, the truth is, we all have stress, fear and obstacles to face. What we need is access to a rescuer who doesn't ever have to pause in order to confront her own troubles.

What we have is better than a knight on a white horse. God is our rescuer, completely invested in our troubles and committed to saving us from that which harms, terrifies or worries us. He is here for today's troubles and He is already on the way to fighting off tomorrow's troubles, with us and for us. We can be rescued – we *will* be rescued!

BODY MATTERS

Give your bodies to God because of all He has done for you. Let them be a living and holy sacrifice – the kind He will find acceptable. This is truly the way to worship Him.

ROMANS 12:1

Fried chicken, cheesy potatoes and a giant glass of soda while spending the evening on the couch watching TV may be a relaxing activity. What if we repeat a similar routine the next night, and the night after that? Is that so bad?

Well, yes. The things we put into our body and the movements (or stillness) we practice are ways in which we worship God. It's not wrong to indulge in a rich meal or spend a lazy evening at home every once in a while, but we need to pay attention to how we treat our bodies, because they are God-created for and God-given to each of us, specifically.

When we remain unaware of the ways in which we are treating our body, we are communicating that we hold little worth in the amazing and unique body God gifted us with. Worship Him by honoring your earthly body!

February 12

Mallory Larsen

OUR SERVANT-KING

*Since He Himself has gone through
suffering and testing, He is able to
help us when we are being tested.*

HEBREWS 2:18

How maddening when an authority figure expects her followers to face circumstances she is exempt from. It can be pretty hard to maintain respect and loyalty to the person (or people) in leadership when they require others to do things they would not.

How does it change things to remember that our God, in the body of Jesus Christ, was a suffering servant? He created the heavens and the earth – *and* He has faced temptation, cruelty and murder. Because of this, we may better relate to God in our struggles because He has been there too!

God knows how hard it can be to walk as a human on this earth, and *because* He knows the reality of it, He is all the more equipped to walk with us through the highs and lows!

STAIR STEPPING

*Faith is the confidence that what we
hope for will actually happen; it gives us
assurance about things we cannot see.*

HEBREWS 11:1

You're walking down the staircase in your home at night, without any lights on. You take each step slowly, holding on to the wall or the railing next to you. You *know* that there are stairs leading all the way down, but may be afraid that you'll miss one or slip and fall.

Similarly, holding on to our faith in God can be scary. Having faith in Him means that we keep taking the next step, even if we cannot see where it is or where it is leading.

In this life, we might (actually, we *will!*) miss a step, we may trip and fall, we may get off course, but we can trust that there will *always* be steps ahead of us and God with us, guiding us to solid ground, so long as we hold on to our faith that He is here.

February 14

THE ULTIMATE MEMBERSHIP

*"Anyone who believes in Me may
come and drink! For the Scriptures declare,
'Rivers of living water will flow from his heart.'"*

JOHN 7:38

Have you ever seen a sign declaring something like, "FOR MEMBERS ONLY"? Maybe it was outside of a restaurant, a swimming pool or a special lounge at the airport. Being a member of nearly any organization typically means that there are perks involved.

While being a member of God's kingdom isn't quite as exclusive as a country club might be, it definitely has its perks for those who want to join. God promises life for those who believe in Him – not just this life, but everlasting life, long after our earthly bodies have failed us.

It's the membership perk beyond all membership perks. This isn't a free meal or an expedited line; this is real and authentic forgiveness of our sins, and life eternal in the perfect bliss of heaven. Can you think of a better membership bonus than that?

February 15

LIFE LESSONS

The kind of sorrow God wants us to experience leads us away from sin and results in salvation.

2 CORINTHIANS 7:10

"So what did you learn from this?"

Oftentimes, when we make a mistake, a caretaker may ask us what lesson we're taking from our misstep. While this may have felt like a formality when being punished in our younger years, it's actually a question God wants us to be asking throughout our lives, because the reality is – He can and does use our sin to move us toward salvation.

Sin is not only something we are to repent from, it is something that can teach us and bolster our walk with God, as we taste the shamefulness, pain or grief of our sinful nature.

While this doesn't (and shouldn't) make sin any more fun or appealing, it can encourage us to know that our sin is not the end of the story. Our walk with God can strengthen, even in our wrongdoings!

February 16

BE LOUD!

Shout to the Lord, all the earth; break out in praise and sing for joy! Sing your praise to the Lord with the harp, with the harp and melodious song, with trumpets and the sound of the ram's horn. Make a joyful symphony before the Lord, the King!

PSALM 98:4-6

Do you ever sing while you're in the shower or driving somewhere in your car? Do you whistle while you're doing housework or keep the beat with a catchy commercial on TV? What about cheering at a sporting event or yelling lyrics at a concert?

We human beings were created to make noise! We can do it in so many various ways, with a soundtrack or without, in a group or by ourselves. And you know what? God loves to hear the sounds we create – always and especially when they are noises being created to praise Him!

We don't need to be at church, with an instrument or in a group to worship God through sound. We can yell! Clap our hands! Snap our fingers! Play the drums on our kitchen counter! Praise His Holy name loudly, proudly and creatively, wherever you can!

NO BUTS!

Be satisfied with what you have. For God has
said, "I will never fail you. I will never abandon you."

HEBREWS 13:5

"I know God says He will never leave me, *but* …"

Have you had thoughts similar to this one before? There's a lot of unbelief wrapped up in the three letters of "b-u-t." If we believe God will never leave us, why can't the sentence end there?

Well, life can be scary sometimes. None of us want to be out of money, without a home or lacking food. Also, many of us wouldn't mind a larger house, more financial security and nicer cars. When, though, is "enough" actually enough?

What thoughts are wrapped up in our unbelief of "b-u-t?" "But, what if I can't pay my rent next month?" Or, "But, I want to live in the nicer neighborhood!" Whatever direction the rest of that sentence takes for each of us, let's consider being satisfied with, "I know God says He will never leave me." Try it! Live in the gratefulness of His presence – it is "enough."

February 18

WHEN THE GOING GETS EASY

I took care of you in the wilderness, in that dry
and thirsty land. But when you had eaten and
were satisfied, you became proud and forgot Me.

HOSEA 13:5-6

What do you do when "the going gets tough," as they say? Do you lean on God and His promises? Do you call on Him for help and comfort?

That is an important question for us to consider but, on the other side of the coin, what do we do when things *are* going our way? We feel happy, healthy and provided for, encouraged by the circumstances and relationships in our life. Does our need for God's help, comfort and promises remain?

We may (and hopefully will!) meet seasons in our lives when we feel like we can stand on our own two feet, but that doesn't mean we cannot still lean on God. His presence and promises are true, in times of difficulty and times of flourishing. Our need for God should not change just because our practical needs don't feel so immediate. Lean in to Him, when you feel like you're falling *and* when you feel like you are standing solidly!

LIFELONG TRAINING

*When troubles of any kind come your way, consider it
an opportunity for great joy. For you know that when
your faith is tested, your endurance has a chance to grow.*

JAMES 1:2-3

For nearly all of us, it is not feasible to simply wake up one morning and run a full marathon. We need to condition our bodies, gradually working our runs up to the length of a full marathon. It requires patience, commitment and a great deal of hard work!

Throughout the training process, our muscles would ache, our breathing would be labored and our body would grow exhausted. There may be days when we simply cannot reach our goal or we might face injuries and setbacks during training. This, however, is when we not only learn our limitations, but we can take patient care in overcoming the hardships of training.

It is not much different in our faith journey. We will feel stretched, sometimes feeling like we're doing the impossible, but each experience, be it a setback or a triumph, is conditioning our spirituality to be better equipped for the journey!

SHOW & TELL

*"Your love for one another will prove
to the world that you are My disciples."*

JOHN 13:35

In what ways do you communicate your faith in God to others? Do you tell them that you are a Christ-follower? Carry your Bible with you? Wear clothing promoting Christian messages? These are not bad things, but "showing" can often be far more powerful than "telling."

Loving people as Jesus did (and does!) not only communicates our commitment to Him, but it impacts the lives of others in a positive way. When we bring food to the hungry, water to the thirsty or a hug to the lonely, we are not only telling them, through our actions, that we are a disciple of Christ, but we are showing them what it looks like to be a follower of Christ.

We are making a difference in their lives, a difference that is love-soaked and selfless, which is what it means to tell others about our faith in God – start by showing them!

February 21

THE GREAT 24-HOUR CYCLE

Great is His faithfulness; His
mercies begin afresh each morning.

LAMENTATIONS 3:23

It's tough when, right from the start of the day, one thing after another goes wrong – *all day long*. After a particularly bad day, it feels almost laughable that we would actually get up the next morning to face *another* day. Why would we want to do that!?

Here's the good news about bad days: they end. Night falls, we rest our weary mind and body, and then, by the grace of God, the sun comes up again in the morning. It is a brand-new day on the calendar, one that the world has never seen before. The memory of the prior day remains, but we can get out of bed and face a new day *because* it is a *brand-new day!*

That doesn't necessarily make it easy to face, but *what if* this day holds good surprises, unforeseen blessings and bold glimpses of the Divine? Maybe yesterday was painful, but today is brand new!

February 22

PURPOSEFUL "ACCIDENTS"

*Remember, it is sin to know what
you ought to do and then not do it.*

JAMES 4:17

Can you imagine getting into a car accident with someone who, after slamming into your vehicle, told you that they had actually done it on purpose? That actually would be no accident, after all! It sounds ridiculous, like real life bumper cars, that anyone would do such a thing intentionally.

It is one thing to do something wrong by accident, but what about the misbehavior we consciously, or even deliberately, engage in? While willfully hitting another car with our own sounds outrageous, it is similar to knowingly engaging in sinful acts. We are imperfect beings who will undoubtedly make mistakes, but there are some missteps that we *can* avoid. Being aware of what sin is gives us the opportunity to avoid that behavior.

Let's take the opportunity to live up to higher standards, steering clear of intentional bumper car moments!

BYPASSING
THE EASY ROUTE

If we endure hardship, we will reign with Him.

2 Timothy 2:12

Have you ever heard the old adage that nothing worthwhile is ever easy? It's sort of maddening, isn't it? Why can't good and worthwhile things ever be totally effortless?!

While that may always be in question, it's hard to argue that an eternal life with Christ is not worthy of some struggle. What better payoff for our troubles than to forever live with the Creator of the Universe? We may find that some things simply are not worth the effort, but as we experience difficulties in Christian living, hold on to the truth of what is coming.

We may be persecuted, feel lonely or struggle to keep our faith at the forefront of our lives, but in the end, we will be with God in His heavenly kingdom. The difficulties of this life may turn out to be only small blips in the grander picture of our eternity with God.

February 24

PAUSING TO LISTEN

Don't look out only for your own
interests, but take an interest in others, too.

PHILIPPIANS 2:4

How are you?

How often do you greet someone with this – *and* wait to hear the answer? It is kind to be curious about how another person is doing, but the real kindness is offered when the curiosity is genuine enough that their response is actually important to us.

It feels honoring when someone asks how we are *and* waits around to listen to an answer deeper than, "I'm fine." In the same respect, we can honor those around us by pausing for their response. Doing so elevates others above ourselves, communicating that we are interested in more than just our own wellbeing, which is a Christ-like way to be in relationship with others.

We never know what stories we might be told when we wait to hear how another person is doing. Those stories could move us to action on behalf of another, creating life-altering moments for someone in need – all because we paused to listen!

February 25

THE NOT-SO-UNFORGIVEABLE

*"Though your sins are like scarlet,
I will make them as white as snow."*

ISAIAH 1:18

Have you ever committed a sin that you thought you simply could not recover from? It was *too* bad, *too* shameful, *too* severe, *too* ugly or unforgiveable.

Life is dark when we cannot imagine forgiving ourselves, let alone receiving forgiveness from other people – *and* from God. It feels like we've exhausted grace and will be marked by the shamefulness of this sin forever.

These moments, however, are when we are invited to glimpse the unfathomable goodness of our Savior. His grace cannot be exhausted. We cannot cross a line of our sin where, suddenly, we are *too* bad, shameful, severe, ugly or unforgiveable. While we may need to do the work of learning how to forgive ourselves, His forgiveness is readily available. Can we accept it? Can we let His light in during our darkest moments? He thinks we're worthy enough to live free from being forever marked by our sin – may we believe that, too.

February 26

Mallory Larsen

NOT ALONE

Be strong and courageous, and do the work.
Don't be afraid or discouraged, for the LORD God,
my God, is with you. He will not fail you or forsake you.
He will see to it that all the work … is finished correctly.

1 CHRONICLES 28:20

Work can pile up. There are numerous tasks at our job, things to do at home and responsibilities in our communities and relationships. Sometimes it feels like the amount of work to be done is not *simply* a pile, but a mountain much bigger than we, or our abilities, measure. Feeling overwhelmed often goes hand-in-hand with hopelessness. When we have so much to do that we don't know where to begin, it's easy to just *not* begin.

God is in the day-to-day parts of our lives that include to-do lists and gigantic projects. When we feel overwhelmed with a project, *God is there*. When we are feeling weary, in our soul or in our body, God, too, is there. No matter how overwhelmed we feel, we can take a deep breath and look at one "to-do list" item at a time, knowing we're not going to do it alone!

CONTAGIOUS ATTITUDES

A cheerful heart is good medicine, but
a broken spirit saps a person's strength.

PROVERBS 17:22

If complaining was difficult, do you think anyone would actually do it? It's incredibly easy to spout out complaints or express negativity about matters of life that are both trivial and significant! For many of us, complaining takes nearly no effort, while speaking positive or encouraging words sometimes requires us to dig a little deeper in how we view a situation, particularly that which is challenging or uncomfortable.

The thing about complaining, however, is that it can so easily suck the goodness of life out of our life! Nearly nobody wants to be around a perpetually negative person (Do you?).

Consistent antagonism colors every situation a shade so dark that, soon, no one can even see the light anymore. It becomes virtually impossible to recognize the goodness in the circumstance and, therefore, makes it hard to see God in it. As we speak positive words, we can be a bearer of light and encouragement for others – and ourselves!

THE POWER TO INCITE

Fire goes out without wood, and
quarrels disappear when gossip stops.

PROVERBS 26:20

There are some things that continue to take effect without human provocation, such as the rotation of the earth or the law of gravity. Other things, however, require our incitement. Our bodies need food and water to live, cars need gasoline to run and lights need electricity to turn on.

Similarly, gossip and slander need our provocation in order to spread. Without our participation, gossip cannot live in our relationships and communities. When we hold our tongues and remain intentional in speaking kind words to and about others, gossip suffocates; it simply cannot live on without our incitement.

This truth grants us with a great deal of power, knowing that we are the ones who can give life to gossip, or take it away. What will we do with this responsibility – fan the flames of gossip or extinguish them?

March

SMALL ACTS, GREAT KINDNESS

*Make the most of every
opportunity in these evil days.*

EPHESIANS 5:16

Turn on the news, read through a list of prayer requests or observe how we treat each other in a traffic jam. It's a good thing we have hope in God for a future of goodness, because so many people in this hurting world are being deprived of joy every single day. We are living in a sad state of affairs.

But *we are here* – active individuals who contribute, for better or for worse, to the state of our communities. We may not be able to take away the pain, fear or grief of another, but we can do little things to communicate care, friendliness and God's love to others.

Letting someone go ahead of us in the checkout line or leaving a small note of encouragement on the desk of a co-worker are little actions that don't require much of us, but can bring forth light in the midst of dark days.

March 1

STOPPING FOR DIRECTIONS

If you need wisdom, ask our generous
God, and He will give it to you.

JAMES 1:5

Do you ever feel like you have gone a bit astray – overwhelmed with numerous routes you could take to get on course, literally or figuratively, but not knowing which one would be best?

Life is filled with countless decisions; some are larger than others, but each shapes the direction of our journey. While many of us might like to think that we are capable of making both the assumedly substantial and seemingly mundane decisions on our own, without hesitation, it simply isn't always that easy. We need wisdom in our decision-making – Divine wisdom that can offer clarity to our clouded minds.

When facing decisions that require wisdom deeper than the capacity of our own mind, we can ask God for help! Let's ask Him to instill wisdom in us – to make clear the path that we should travel. He delights in guiding our way!

March 2

BEAUTY SURROUNDS

*The sun has one kind of glory, while the moon
and stars each have another kind. And even
the stars differ from each other in their glory.*

1 CORINTHIANS 15:41

There is, surely, only one person on this earth that you find to be beautiful, correct? You could only name one person in the world who you consider to be successful, funny or athletic? Right?

That would not only be ridiculous, but quite limiting, wouldn't it? How could any of us consider the vastness of seven billion people, yet only see *one* (or even two, or three, or one thousand!) as being beautiful, intelligent or talented? It is all too easy to compare ourselves to others – to see the beauty, success or wisdom of another person and then feel discouraged about what we lack (or, what we have, but cannot see!).

There is obviously not only *one* attractive or talented person inhabiting the earth – there are countless! We each exhibit beauty, intelligence and gifts in ways as numerous as the population. We can notice the beauty and unique giftedness in those around us, but let us not forget to see it in *ourselves*, too!

March 3

WORTH THE WAIT

*This vision is for a future time. It describes
the end, and it will be fulfilled. If it seems
slow in coming, wait patiently, for it will
surely take place. It will not be delayed.*

HABAKKUK 2:3

Do you ever spend wild amounts of time making a great meal? The thing about the *perfect* meal is that there is no question that it will take a great deal of time to create. Shortening the amount of time that the bread needs to bake or the meat needs to marinate will just negatively affect the taste of the final product.

What is God cultivating within you that needs time to marinate? Maybe it is a specific talent, the fulfillment of a vision or a desired relationship. It's difficult to wait, especially when we are not sure how *long* we'll be waiting, but when the "marinating" is complete and the vision is fulfilled, we just might see, in retrospect, what was happening in and around us during the waiting period.

We don't want to eat half-baked bread or uncooked meat – take heart, because such goodness can be produced during our patient waiting!

March 4

EYES TO SEE

Ever since the world was created, people have seen the earth and sky. Through everything God made, they can clearly see His invisible qualities – His eternal power and divine nature. So they have no excuse for not knowing God.

ROMANS 1:20

Where do you notice God? Do you become aware of His presence while in church or feel His nearness when you read Scripture? Maybe you see God's existence while walking in nature or listening to a beautiful composition of music.

The amazing part about the gift of God's presence is that all we need to do is open our eyes and look around – there He is! He created the trees, the flowers, the animals and the mountains; we can notice Him in those creations. He made the faces we pass on the street and the sky we do life under, day in and day out. He designed the sun that shines on our faces and the rain that falls on our head.

When we are struggling to find God, let's take a moment to notice that which is all around us. He created this! When God feels distant, take comfort in seeing that His handiwork surrounds us!

SOUL WORKOUTS

*Physical training is good, but training
for godliness is much better, promising
benefits in this life and in the life to come.*

1 TIMOTHY 4:8

Exercise is an excellent way to honor and care for our bodies. Having a regular routine, whether at a gym, at home or outside, is a kind way of being mindful and supportive of our health. What practices do you have to take care of your body?

In a similar, though more eternal, fashion, we can partake in spiritual practices, which will exercise, strengthen and promote the health of our faith. This is a regular routine that can take place in a church, at home or outside (or maybe in all three places), and the impact is timeless.

Unlike the exercise we give our physical body, which will, inevitably, one day fail us, our spiritual practices guide us into our everlasting life in heaven.

What practices do you have to take care of your soul?

March 6

OUT OF CONTROL!

He existed before anything else,
and He holds all creation together.

COLOSSIANS 1:17

It's pretty comforting to feel like we are in control of a situation, isn't it? When we think we hold the power, then we think we can direct the outcome!

What, however, happens when things start to unravel? Maybe we thought we had control, but the *illusion* of control is suddenly revealed and we start to feel the chaos and overwhelm of a now-messy and uncontrolled happening. In the midst of all the commotion, we'd like to hand over all of the pieces to someone who can create order out of disorder.

When we find ourselves disillusioned by the illusion of control, let's remember who really holds all of the pieces to begin with. It should bring all the more comfort to know that we aren't actually in control, but God, who created every inch of the earth and the creatures who inhabit it, can call the shots – and, ultimately, we *want* Him to!

March 7

LESS TALKING, MORE WALKING

If anyone claims, "I am living in the light," but hates a fellow believer, that person is still living in darkness.

1 JOHN 2:9

Have you ever been told that it's not *just* about "talking the talk," but also about "walking the walk?" This, in short, means that our actions should match our words. We may often hear this discussed in the matter of politics. Which candidate is going to "walk the walk," so to speak? It can be easy for him or her to tell us all of their beliefs and grand plans, but once elected, will their actions match their promises?

To call ourselves a Christian is a brave, bold and honorable claim to make, but our "talk" must be followed up by a "walk" that speaks just as loudly. How are we "walking the walk" today? In what ways are we supporting our words through our actions? If we profess ourselves as Christian and then withhold love from another, boast about our own character or judge others cruelly, we negate our own confession of following Christ. Let's allow our "walk" to do the talking!

March 8

PRICELESS ACCESSORIES

Above all, clothe yourselves with love,
which binds us all together in perfect harmony.

COLOSSIANS 3:14

Is there an article of clothing or an accessory that you hate to leave the house without? Maybe it's a meaningful piece of jewelry, a favorite bag or a comfortable sweater. Maybe it has become something that others associate with you, leaving them wondering where your watch is when they see you without it on your wrist!

Can you imagine if people associated each of us with something even more beautiful or meaningful than an accessory or clothing item? What if, when people saw us, they were certain that they would also, then, see love in the flesh? What if we so regularly brought joy, laughter, selflessness or kindness to others that, soon, they associated us with something that meaningful and godly?

As we put on our favorite necklace, hat or pair of shoes, think, too, about what it might look like to adorn ourselves with gratitude, peace or servanthood. Let's wear it boldly!

March 9

DON'T HIDE, BUT SEEK

If you look for Me wholeheartedly, you will find Me.

JEREMIAH 29:13

Do you remember playing epic games of *Hide & Go Seek* as a child? There were few things as satisfying as finding the ultimate hiding spot, making it nearly impossible for anybody to find you.

Can you imagine if life with God was like a game of *Hide & Go Seek*? Sometimes it feels that way. We look high and low, far and wide, genuinely desiring to find Him, wholeheartedly seeking to be in His presence.

To God, though, our relationship with Him is no game. He doesn't look for the most unthinkable hiding spot and then wait as we run past Him countless times. Instead, He tells us that He has no good hiding spot. When we seek Him, we will find Him. It will be the shortest game of *Hide & Go Seek* we have ever played!

March 10

LOVE IN OBEDIENCE

"If you love Me, obey My commandments."

JOHN 14:15

How does it feel when a friend or loved one doesn't listen to your desires? What about when your child or employee doesn't honor your instructions or obey your rules? It's understandable that we would feel disrespected and small in those moments. This would feel particularly painful with our partner or child – the ones we consider to be our closest loved one or, literally, our own flesh and blood.

What a blatant rejection, not only of our authority and voice, but also of our worthiness in the relationship.

How painful, then, for our Maker when we disregard His desires or commands? One way we can communicate our love for God is to listen when He speaks and honor what it is that He says. How much love are we showing to Him when we brush off His instructions, as if they aren't worthy of our obedience.

To love God is to listen to God – we honor Him by how we hear and obey!

March 11

A COMMUNITY UNITED

If one part suffers, all the parts suffer with it,
and if one part is honored, all the parts are glad.

1 CORINTHIANS 12:26

Have you ever had a toothache – that *one* tooth that throbs with a pain nearly indescribable? The ache of one tooth can make our entire body feel ill. Our immune system then perks up and begins fighting against infection or the spread of illness.

This is how it should be with the body of Christ. When one person feels discouraged, grieved or hurt, it affects all of us. We all, then, rally around the aching person to fight for healing and health. Similarly, when one person experiences joy and gladness, it should spread like wildfire throughout the community. Their joy can be our joy, and we should embrace it wholeheartedly; and, at times, their pain will be our pain, and we will honor it wholeheartedly.

Then, when our own happiness or aching comes, and it will, others will share in it with us, as one body, united in Christ.

March 12

SPILLING SECRETS

*Finally, I confessed all my sins to You and
stopped trying to hide my guilt. I said to
myself, "I will confess my rebellion to the
Lord." And You forgave me! All my guilt is gone.*

PSALM 32:5

Keeping a secret from someone is hard work, especially when the secret involves our own admission of guilt. Sure, it might seem easier to keep it from them than to confess what we've done, but the guilt associated with the secret can be so substantial that it weighs down on us like a ton of bricks. The effort required in intentionally keeping a secret could consume us for years.

What if our confession won't lead to the outcome we're expecting? What if, on the other side of our admission of guilt, there is freedom – freedom from the shame, guilt and consumption of the sin and the secret. Maybe we're withholding something from a friend or family member, maybe we're withholding it from God, or maybe we're keeping it from both, but we have the promise of God's grace and forgiveness. May we let that promise lead us to confession, and embrace the freedom that awaits!

March 13

LOOKALIKES

The Lord – who is the Spirit – makes
us more and more like Him as we
are changed into His glorious image.

2 CORINTHIANS 3:18

Do you and your friends dress similarly? Do you like to shop at the same stores and embrace a similar fashion sense? What about on a wider scale – do you see various cultures and people groups dressing in similar types of clothing, wearing their hair in similar styles and adorning similar accessories? It is not uncommon for us to look, dress or act in a way that resembles those we live around and spend time with.

The more time we spend with God, the more we are transformed in His image. We might begin to speak like Him or act like Him, leading us to look more like Him!

It's fun to share clothing and music with our friends, but how much more remarkable and gratifying to also share characteristics with the Holy One!

March 14

GIFTS OF LOVE

*Prophecy and speaking in unknown
languages and special knowledge will
become useless. But love will last forever!*

1 Corinthians 13:8

What do you like to study, practice or perform? Do you have special hobbies or gifts that you delight in perfecting and sharing? How wonderful it is to cultivate and offer out our talents for others to experience! Our gifts are a good and beautiful thing, and they should be embraced and used heartily!

In the midst of offering our individual talents to those around us, let us cover them in love. If we share our gift of music, cooking or business management with others, but don't do so in love, then we aren't using our ability to make an eternal impact on others.

Our gifts are a vessel through which we can love others – envelope your skills in love for God and others, and see how it can transform into an everlasting offering!

OUR "HELP" IS HEARD

I cried out to Him for help, praising Him as I spoke.

PSALM 66:17

It is a painful and scary moment when we find ourselves needing to yell for help. Getting to the point of crying out typically means that we are at the end of our rope, feeling helpless and nearly hopeless. We are admitting that we cannot save ourselves, and we are in desperate need of an intervention.

What is simultaneously terrifying and hopeful about calling out for help is the belief that there *is someone who will hear us.* When we scream, we trust that someone may hear and, therefore, that we will be saved.

God's presence surrounds us, no matter how isolated we feel (or literally are) on earth. Our cries to God can simultaneously be praises – we cry out because we trust that He can hear. We ask for His help, and believe, even with only an ounce of our being, that He can step in and save us.

And, He can.

March 16

NO TAGBACKS

Don't say, "I will get even for this wrong."
Wait for the LORD to handle the matter.

PROVERBS 20:22

When another person disappoints us, betrays our trust or breaks our heart, it can be maddening, unfair and agonizing to feel so victimized, while the perpetrator is seemingly free from the deep heartache of the circumstance.

The thought that we will feel better if the person who incites the pain then experiences it themselves is an attractive and convincing message, but it is certainly not a godly one.

We are not ultimately responsible for their convictions, or for creating consequences for their actions. Not only are we not responsible for this, but we can consider it a *freedom* from responsibility! We have our own grief and pain to overcome, and our energy doesn't need to go towards putting others through the pain they pushed us into.

Let God take over in that arena – we don't have to bother with revenge!

HUMANITY UNITED

What gives you the right to make such a judgment? What do you have that God hasn't given you? And if everything you have is from God, why boast as though it were not a gift?

1 CORINTHIANS 4:7

What goes through your head when you see a homeless person asking for money as you walk down the street? Do you wonder about their story or make assumptions about their abilities? It can be difficult not to jump to conclusions about those we pass by who beg for us to share our blessings.

What, though, would we see if we look into their eyes? What stories could we hear, what lessons could we learn from any of the strangers we pass by or interact with each day? Can we allow ourselves to open up to those who need help? Can we wonder about their lives and share with them our God-given blessings? Their life experiences may be wildly different from ours, but they feel pain, fear and shame just as we do. In fact, our stories may not be as different as we think – let's share in both the pain and joy of our humanity together.

March 18

CHANGING SEASONS

The one sitting on the throne said,
"Look, I am making all things new!"

REVELATION 21:5

Hope is wrapped up in the changing seasons. Summer, so full of life, slowly shifts into the vividness of autumn. By the time winter arrives, the leaves have fallen from the trees, plants have died and hibernation is in full swing.

The world looks faded and the light of each day is all too swift. *And then* (herein lies the hopeful part), *spring comes!* The sun shines for a little bit longer, flowers bloom and bright green leaves reappear on the trees – new life is formed!

Year after year, like clockwork, we see old life fade and new life appear. Hope can be found in knowing that while we may sometimes feel like we're in the midst of a never-ending season of winter, *spring is coming.* God promises to make all things new! We see Him fulfill that promise for our landscape each year, and we can trust that He will fulfill it for our soul, as well!

March 19

NOTICING GOODNESS

To enjoy your work and accept your lot
in life – this is indeed a gift from God.

ECCLESIASTES 5:19

Consider how you spend your days. Do you work a job simply to pay your bills, counting down the hours until each workday is complete? Maybe you save the weekends for living your life, while the weekdays are simply to be survived.

It is good to fulfill our responsibilities and work a job that supports us and our family, but it is a shame when we cannot enjoy that which fills our time. While there may be seasons when our job is less than desirable, we're overwhelmed with all that is on our plate or we're stressed about not having *enough* on our plate, joy is available when we can recognize what we *do* have. How do you allow any antipathy to rob you of gratitude and joy for what you do have?

Let's focus on what we have, rather than what we don't (or what we want to change!). What's good with you today?!

March 20

MINDFUL GENEROSITY

*You must each decide in your heart
how much to give. And don't give
reluctantly or in response to pressure.*

2 CORINTHIANS 9:7

A man smiles kindly at you as he rings a bell for donations outside of the grocery store; a woman working with a clothing drive calls to ask if you'll have anything to give during their next pickup; missionaries in need of financial assistance are visiting your church, hoping to raise support for their work; a child rings your doorbell, selling magazines to raise money for his education.

BIG SIGH. We are never without a number of individuals and organizations vying for our donations. We are called to be generous with our money, giving to those in need, but discernment is still a factor in this process.

We should be good stewards of our money, which means we are mindful of how much and how often we are giving to others. To give without any measure of wisdom or discernment may lead us to give for the wrong reasons or to the wrong people.

THE NEED FOR "WE"

"My grace is all you need.
My power works best in weakness."

2 CORINTHIANS 12:9

Teamwork is a wonderful thing. When we can work together to complete a project, rather than going about it alone, we can experience the satisfaction of completion without our own personal resources being completely exhausted. We were meant to do life with others, to help and be helped. At what point, however, in our own personal journeys do we find ourselves needing to stop and ask for help? How helpless must we feel before we bring in reinforcements?

When we can recognize our limitations, the help that is available becomes more accessible. If we *know* that we, alone, are incapable of going about something on our own, we can invite both God and others into the project before we become exhausted or overwhelmed. When we can say that a task needs to be done by "we," and not "I," then the task is *already* easier – before it has even begun!

March 22

WHEN THE MIRROR IS IN CONTROL

*Your heart was filled with pride
because of all your beauty. Your wisdom
was corrupted by your love of splendor.*

EZEKIEL 28:17

How many times a day do you find yourself looking in a mirror? Do you take and retake "selfies" until you have the perfect shot? What length of time does it take for you to get ready each morning? In short, do you ever wonder how much of our lives is spent thinking about or enhancing our appearance?!

It is good to feel confident and beautiful in our bodies, but when our desire for those good feelings begins to overtake us, becoming more important than many other things, then we're chasing after pride and fleeting fulfillment.

Today, let's wonder if our appearance is dictating our values. May we love what we see when we look in the mirror, but may we focus more deeply on what cannot be seen in that reflection. Let's pamper our fruits of the Spirit with care and tenderness as we prepare for each day!

UNTYING THE BLINDFOLD

When He saw the crowds, He had compassion
on them because they were confused and
helpless, like sheep without a shepherd.

MATTHEW 9:36

Do you ever feel like you are walking through life blindfolded, uncertain about where you are headed or how you will ever get there? Some life circumstances are so complicated or chaotic that it can be overwhelming to try to navigate our way through the web of feelings, relationships, values and practicalities. Maybe we're feeling blindfolded and helpless in a maze of worry and confusion. Those are scary times.

The blindfold, however, can be removed. We don't have to navigate on our own, no matter the circumstance. When we don't know where we're going, we're unsure of how to get there or we simply don't want to journey alone – let God remove the blindfold and lead the way. Can you hear Him whispering directions? Can you feel Him guiding you? Look! See! He's here!

March 24

SMALL VALUABLES

"If you are faithful in little things, you will be faithful in large ones. But if you are dishonest in little things, you won't be honest with greater responsibilities."

LUKE 16:10

With many things in life, we must start small. We crawl before we walk, listen before we can speak and practice before we perform. Our jobs and relationships, too, typically require modest beginnings. To prove our abilities and trustworthiness to others (and to have it proven to us), we must start somewhere and, usually, the small places are where to begin. Why would our boss trust us with a substantial project when we haven't shown her that we can (and will) do the smaller tasks, such as respond to an email promptly or show up for work on time?

The small things matter, whether they are practical or relational. The little movements we make, the tiny beginnings, are what equip us to do grander things in the future. Let's not discredit the significance of our work in any realm of our lives, for our work is what builds character, expertise and trust. Embrace the small movements!

March 25

THE TRUTH FREES

*This is what you must do: Tell the truth
to each other. Render verdicts in your
courts that are just and that lead to peace.*

ZECHARIAH 8:16

The truth hurts.

That line can oftentimes be used to justify pain, but it is, in itself, a painful sentiment. Is that it? Does the truth *just* hurt us? The truth of something *can* bring us pain, but that is not the whole story. The truth can hurt – and the truth can offer freedom, honor, goodness and fullness of life. When we keep the truth from someone for fear of hurting another, we are not *only* blocking out the possibility of pain. We are also keeping the other from what hopeful things can be possible when we speak the truth.

The truth can hurt, but it can also heal. When we commit to speaking the truth in love, we are creating genuine relationships through our authentic presence in the world. When we are honest with one another, we can build trust and safety in our relationships that invites sincerity from each person we engage!

March 26

GUESS WHAT?!

Never be ashamed to tell others about our Lord.

2 TIMOTHY 1:8

What's your favorite store? Imagine that a close friend heard that store was having a *massive* sale – 99% off everything in the store! This is such good news! What's more, they have somehow managed to increase their inventory to unfathomable levels; it would actually be impossible for the store to run out of stock. It doesn't get any better than this!

Now, what if your friend didn't tell you about the sale? What if they kept this incredible information from you until it was too late? Can you imagine the devastation, anger and betrayal you would feel?!

What's better news than our favorite store having an unthinkable sale? God's saving grace! Who needs to hear about who doesn't know yet? Who are we holding this back from – and will we share our excitement with them today?

March 27

DID YOU HEAR ME?

*We must listen very carefully to the truth
we have heard, or we may drift away from it.*

HEBREWS 2:1

You're in school, at work or about to embark on a grand adventure – all places where instructions, warnings and helpful tips are offered regularly. Do you ever find yourself simply zoning out? Maybe you're tired or have too many other things on your mind; maybe you think you have all of the information you need, so listening to further instruction seems senseless.

Regardless of what keeps us from listening to instructions, it is generally not helpful for us to tune them out. When we're always zoning out during the offering of instructions, what we have heard in the past may fade or we could miss some genuinely helpful information.

The same is true for the instructions we receive through Scripture and biblical teachings – no matter how often we've heard it before, let's listen again, keeping God's instructions sounding loudly in our hearts!

March 28

INDESTRUCTIBLE LOVE

"Heaven and earth will disappear,
but My words will never disappear."

MARK 13:31

The destruction after a violent natural disaster is devastating. Have you seen the pictures of a tornado-ravaged town, its homes, buildings and trees lying in ruins? The scene can be ugly, scary and nearly unbelievable. What about, however, that one structure that might survive the storm? The entire town may be flattened, but sometimes there might be one tree, home or park bench that survives the disaster. How can that be? It is such a mystery!

All of the things in this world are fleeting. Someday soon or one day in the distant future, what is here, on this earth, will pass.

The truth of God – His Word and presence – is the single thing that will remain. When all else is flattened, so to speak, God remains standing in a mysterious and beautiful way. This gives us all the more reason to hold on to His truth, because we know that it will survive any storm.

ASKING FOR HELP

*Fools think their own way is
right, but the wise listen to others.*

PROVERBS 12:15

You are lost, driving in an unfamiliar area for a seemingly endless amount of time. You pass by several gas stations and stores, opting not to take the time to stop because, surely, *the correct road is so close by!* After a while, things start looking familiar – not because you've found your way, but because you've driven in a complete circle and are now back where your journey astray first began.

Doesn't it seem silly that one wouldn't stop to ask for directions? Why drive around somewhat aimlessly when there are resources we can tap for help. Plainly put, it is pretty foolish (and prideful) not to seek help when we are lost.

Life can be pretty disorienting sometimes. Whether we're driving in circles in our car or metaphorically running around in circles in our day-to-day life, we would be wise to reach out to others, seeking guidance, wisdom and encouragement for our journey.

March 30

FINDING REST

In peace I will lie down and sleep,
for You alone, O LORD, will keep me safe.

PSALM 4:8

Sometimes it's difficult to shut our brains off, so to speak. When we have a lot going on – work is piling up, our relationships feel strained or we're waiting to hear back from the doctor about test results – it can be incredibly hard to find rest.

Anxiety is a lot of work, and it doesn't tire easily. Our ability to experience deep rest or uninterrupted sleep can be greatly hindered when we're feeling weighed down by the worries of our days.

How much better equipped we are, however, to face challenges when our mind and body are well rested. It is no easy feat to put a pause on our racing thoughts or anxiety for the sake of a restful night, but it is possible. God can take our troubles for the night so we can experience a worry-free sleep – and, if we let Him, He can even hold onto them in the morning, too!

March 31

April

GREAT REWARD IS TO COME

If we are faithful to the end, trusting God
just as firmly as when we first believed,
we will share in all that belongs to Christ.

HEBREWS 3:14

There was once a contest where participants had to keep their hand touching one particular vehicle for as long as they could. They could move their feet or turn their body slightly, but their hand could not lift up from the car, lest they be disqualified. The final contestant to be safe from disqualification would win the car, along with a monetary prize.

Essentially, the contest was calling for commitment, endurance and obedience. It seems like a silly challenge, but it is somewhat comparable to our faith walk.

Living for God means that we must embrace commitment, endurance and obedience for Him. The journey may sometimes be tedious, other times painful and, with hope, often joy-filled. A very grand prize awaits us all who remain dedicated to honoring God and living our lives with and for Him.

SECRET BLESSINGS

"Watch out! Don't do your good deeds
publicly, to be admired by others, for you will
lose the reward from your Father in heaven."

MATTHEW 6:1

It can be really fun to do good and selfless deeds for others. When we buy dinner for the hungry, bring water to the thirsty or give flowers to the hurting, we are doing small acts that bring the Kingdom of God here to earth in beautiful ways.

Because it feels so good to bless someone else, it can be easy to want to share with the world what kind deed we have done. What if, shortly after serving someone, we take to social media in order to share with all of our friends what we have done? Maybe we're bursting with joy or want to encourage others to serve as we have served. Slowly, our selfless deed transforms into a more self-focused celebration of our kindness, which begins to defeat the purpose of serving one another.

Let's serve each other selflessly and remain aware of what we do with the joy we feel afterwards!

April 2

RIGHT WHERE WE ARE

Moses told the people, "Don't be afraid.
Just stand still and watch the LORD rescue you today."

EXODUS 14:13

You are stuck outside in the middle of a storm, being pursued by a predator or caught in the crossfire of conflict. What is your natural inclination? For most of us, we would choose to run – fast and far! When we are afraid, it is easy (and often preferable) to run and hide. This could mean literally running away from a person or circumstance, or it could be that we withdraw or retreat emotionally.

While there are, undoubtedly, particular conditions when running to take cover would be wise, God tells us that in our fears – be it a fear of failure, heartbreak or deep loss – we need not run. We don't need to take cover or retreat from the rest of the world, because God is able to meet us *right* where we are and protect us from our trepidation.

The effort it takes to run is not needed here – we can stay right where we are!

April 3

THE REAL JACKPOT

*The love of money is the root of all kinds
of evil. And some people, craving money,
have wandered from the true faith and
pierced themselves with many sorrows.*

1 TIMOTHY 6:10

What would it be like to win the lottery? Where would you even begin to spend, give or invest your winnings? When we are feeling as if we're drowning in bills, it can be fun to think about the prospect of winning the lottery. What would we ever have to worry about if we had that much money?

What is tough about having more money than we even know what to do with is that there could easily be a loss of authenticity in our lives. Our relationships may become surface-level and our problems may be masked by our influx of income. The love of money, whether it is money we have or only money we desire, takes our focus off of the fruits of the spirit such as joy and peace, which can bring us a happiness far deeper than a growing bank account.

What are the sources of your joy today?

April 4

TAKING RESPONSIBILITY

Put on your new nature, created to
be like God – truly righteous and holy.

EPHESIANS 4:24

What happens when we move out on our own, get married or become a mom? Well, a *lot* of things happen, but one of the primary changes is the shift in our responsibilities. For the most part, there is not much turning back once we enter into these responsibilities. Our life will alter, sometimes dramatically, as we meet the obligations of our changing roles.

The same is true when we commit our lives to Christ. We cannot simply say we are a Christian and then continue living exactly as we were. Being a Christ-follower means that we have different responsibilities than we once did; it means that we live in such a way that others can see our role as a follower of Christ without us ever having to tell them.

What shifts need to occur in your way of being so you can more deeply live as one who honors and follows Christ?

THE VALUE IN LISTENING

Spouting off before listening to the
facts is both shameful and foolish.

PROVERBS 18:13

Your best friend approaches you with relationship problems – again. You are feeling pretty certain that she simply should not be in this relationship anymore; their disputes are plenty and their arguments seem to be repetitive. Every time she comes to you for advice, it sounds like a similar problem she's facing, much like the one you shared advice on the time before, and the time before that *and* the time before that. So, you find yourself listening half-heartedly before going through the same spectacular advice that you always offer.

But what if you miss something this time around? What if she is reaching out with delicate, pertinent information and desperately needs insight and comfort – and you are unable to meet her in the moment because you advised before you listened? We can offer valuable, godly, comforting advice, but we need to put our assumptions aside and listen before we speak into the lives of others!

BUILDING AND REBUILDING

I said to them, "You know very well what trouble we are in.
Jerusalem lies in ruins, and its gates have been destroyed by fire.
Let us rebuild the wall of Jerusalem and end this disgrace!"
Then I told them about how the gracious hand of God had been
on me, and about my conversation with the king. They replied at
once, "Yes, let's rebuild the wall!" So they began the good work.

NEHEMIAH 2:17-18

As we navigate our way through life, it's no secret that we will make mistakes. Some will be bigger than others, but all of them can find repair through God's unending grace. After receiving God's grace, however, the work may not be done. While grace can cover the sin, we should wonder about what other repairs we could do to mend wounds.

Maybe a relationship was broken because of a painful sin committed. Receiving God's grace can restore us in beautiful ways, but we can then consider what sort of restoration we should be doing in the relationship. Can the relationship be rebuilt? Time may tell, but we can at least pick up the pieces and attempt to rebuild – God's grace cleanses us, and we can continue the good work of grace, healing and repair.

April 7

THE SAFEST PLACE

Yet I still dare to hope when I
remember this: The faithful love of the
LORD never ends! His mercies never cease.

LAMENTATIONS 3:21-22

I've had enough. I'm done. I can't take this anymore.

Has anybody ever told you that before, in regards to your relationship? Have you ever told someone that before? Has the strain, conflict and stress of the relationship ever been simply too much to bear? Abandonment and loss of relationship is unspeakably painful – *and* it is a very real risk we take when being in human relationships.

The safety of being in relationship with the Divine One is that we can be certain we will not experience abandonment. We cannot be too much for God. We cannot wear out His grace, patience or desire to stay with us. It is simply not possible. Although it is scary to be in relationships with human beings, who could leave us, it is a safe investment to be in relationship with God.

We can never be too much for Him; He can never get enough of us!

BEARERS OF GOODNESS

All praise to God, the Father of our Lord Jesus Christ.
God is our merciful Father and the source of
all comfort. He comforts us in all our troubles so that
we can comfort others. When they are troubled, we will
be able to give them the same comfort God has given us.

2 CORINTHIANS 1:3-4

When a caretaker puts a cold washcloth on our feverish forehead, a friend brings dinner over when we're overworked or a boss offers us words of encouragement for a job well done, we feel loved and well cared for. We experience the goodness of those acts of kindness and, therefore, know how sweet it will feel for someone else to receive similar compassion from us. We know, particularly well, how to offer kindness when it has first been shown to us.

What acts of kindness have been shown to you that you may, then, pass on to others? What about days when we're feeling emptied of love, struggling in our relationships and lonely in our communities? Can we remember God's generous love for us, and let that flow through us into our relationships? Let's remember what it feels like to be chosen and cared for, and share that goodness with others!

April 9

GOD SPOTS

*You are my hiding place; You protect me from
trouble, You surround me with songs of victory.*

PSALM 32:7

Did you have a go-to spot when you were feeling ashamed, scared or lonely as a child; maybe you slid under your bed, crouched in the bathtub or had a favorite tree you climbed. What about now, as an adult?

It is nice to have a place we can escape to when life feels like too much. What if, however, your place is inaccessible at any given moment, or eventually fails to bring you the same comfort and respite it once did? Anywhere we are – at home or in public, feeling distressed or feeling joy – we can find respite in God. We don't need to be in a particular spot (though it is sometimes nice to have our own special spot!), but we can stop where we are or go with God to our favorite park bench or coffee shop.

It is in Him, rather than our surroundings, that we will feel deep peace!

April 10

STORIES OF HEALING

We can rejoice, too, when we run into problems and trials, for we know that they help us develop endurance. And endurance develops strength of character, and character strengthens our confident hope of salvation. And this hope will not lead to disappointment. For we know how dearly God loves us, because He has given us the Holy Spirit to fill our hearts with His love.

ROMANS 5:3-5

Do you have any scars on your body? What stories do they tell? Do they remind you of scary moments or brave feats? Do they speak of accidents or illness, shame or suffering? Is your scar(s) an ugly or a sweet part of your body?

Each scar tells a story but, more than that, it speaks of survival. Whatever the circumstance that led to the breaking of our skin, its healing says that whatever caused the wound was *not* the end of the story – healing came. In our lives, we will face troubles, temptations and the marring of our own skin. We will struggle, but those struggles will build character; they will define us and they will soon turn into a story of survival. Our troubles will not be the end of the story – God has already written the end, and it is one of healing for us all!

April 11

WELCOMING HELP

Two people are better off than one, for
they can help each other succeed. If one
person falls, the other can reach out and help.
But someone who falls alone is in real trouble.

ECCLESIASTES 4:9-10

Sometimes it feels easier if we just complete a task on our own, without the help of others. Sure, it's nice to have an extra set of hands for nearly any project, but it is easy to think that the process will be quicker if we don't have to pause to instruct somebody else on what needs to be done. We'll just do it ourselves!

Maybe that works for some tasks but, on the whole, *we need each other.* It is good to invite others into our processes and projects, to let ourselves be helped, even when we are completely able.

When we are operating as a community, even when we *could* go about things alone, we'll be more unified during times of strength and weakness!

SELF-INSTRUCTED TIMEOUTS

Don't sin by letting anger control you.
Think about it overnight and remain silent.

PSALM 4:4

Throughout a hockey game, players who lose their temper will be sent to the penalty box as both a punishment and a cool-down. While the hockey players in the penalty box may not totally let go of their anger during their time in the box, the thought behind the penalty box isn't an entirely bad idea.

Our anger can easily control our actions and words; things can escalate quickly and take an ugly turn before we're able to cool down. We may not need an actual "box" to sit in, but we may want to consider the penalty box the next time we're feeling angry. Maybe we should remove ourselves from the situation and take some time to sit, breathe and be quiet. Maybe we need time for our heart to stop pounding and our tight grip to loosen, before returning back to the scene where we can, with a clearer head, better navigate the circumstance causing our anger.

WHAT'S GOING ON!?

Ask Me and I will tell you remarkable
secrets you do not know about things to come.

JEREMIAH 33:3

Have you ever found out information "after the fact" about a friend or loved one? Why didn't you hear anything sooner! Maybe they didn't want to share their news with you – or maybe they didn't tell you because you didn't ask. It could be a promotion at work, a relationship status change or an impending move; whatever the reason for you not hearing the news, it is nice to be informed about things to come in the lives of our loved ones!

What about in our own lives? What sort of conversations are we having with God about what's to come? Do we want to be surprised with big changes in our lives, or can we ask Him about what's to come and let Him reveal the stories of our future to us?

We don't *have* to wait and be shocked at what's to come – ask Him now, and let's listen to how He fills us in!

April 14

UNCONDITIONAL KINDNESS

"Love your enemies! Do good to them.
Lend to them without expecting to be repaid."

LUKE 6:35

When people treat us unkindly, just about the *last* thing we want to do is to bless and serve them. Our natural inclination is often to defend ourselves and to fight back with a strength and steadiness that is not necessarily operating out of love. What if, however, we can respond to unkindness with kindness? What if we bless, even ever so slightly, those who want to see us fail or hurt?

When we cease to reply to bullying with bullying, we're doing a big part in extinguishing the fire that is igniting the cruelty.

We cannot be responsible for what our enemies do with our loving response to their harshness, but we can trust that it is a godly way to engage with their unkindness.

Let them see the love of God, which cannot be shaken by bullying.

April 15

TAKE A PEEK

Don't be selfish; don't try to impress others. Be humble, thinking of others as better than yourselves.

PHILIPPIANS 2:3

Do you ever find yourself "people watching" as you sit in an airport, restaurant or shopping mall? It can be entertaining to witness snippets of others' lives and conversations, but what conclusions do those snippets lead us to make?

What if we elevated our view of others in such a way that we remain aware of how vast each person's story is? How can we have eyes to see others, both strangers and loved ones, as God sees them? Well, to start, we need to remember that the window through which we see a person's life, be it for 3 minutes or 30 years, is just that – a window.

There is an entire soul in another, one that we cannot fully know; but to believe that God treasures that soul is an honorable reminder of how precious each life we peek into really is.

PASSING TIME

*A hard worker has plenty of food, but a
person who chases fantasies has no sense.*

PROVERBS 12:11

How do you spend your free time? Do you know the hours in a day that you give to social media, television or surfing the Internet? What sort of productivity is being dismissed for the sake of moments passed in front of a screen?

It is good to give our minds and bodies a chance to rest, but there is a fine line between resting time and wasted time. When activities that give us a chance to catch our breath or rest our minds become a glorified focus of the day, eating up minutes that could be spent honoring our passions or responsibilities, then that which colors our unique presence in the world becomes a little bit duller. Our potential fades, even if only slightly.

May we honor our need for rest while continuing to pursue what it is we were put on this earth to do, adding our own bursting colors to the landscape of our world!

April 17

CONSISTENT OBEDIENCE, SPONTANEOUS ADVENTURES

*Jesus called out to them, "Come, follow Me,
and I will show you how to fish for people!"
And they left their nets at once and followed Him.*

MATTHEW 4:19-20

Obedience can be tricky, especially when our obedience calls us to do things we simply do not want to do! Maybe if we pretend we couldn't hear displeasing instructions, then they will just go away and a more convenient or desirable call to obedience will come around for us!

Living in obedience to God may mean that we literally drop what we're doing at any given moment to follow Him on what may seem like a wild, outrageous or confusing path. Could you do that?

How tightly are you holding on to aspects of your life such as your job, place of residence or relationships? What if, today, God asked you to make a significant life change? We must wonder – is our commitment to being obedient to God greater than our commitment to the conditions of our life?

April 18

WORDS WITH MEANING

"Even if that person wrongs you seven times a day and each time turns again and asks forgiveness, you must forgive."

LUKE 17:4

"I'm sorry" is a phrase that is meant to hold a great deal of meaning, remorse and authenticity, though it is so easy for most of us to spout it out to others as a formality rather than a genuine apology.

How do you respond when an "I'm sorry" is quickly tossed in your direction with, seemingly, little meaning? Maybe a short time later, another hurried "Sorry!" is offered to you – and then another. It is fair to say that we may soon tire from these apathetic apologies. And, yet, we are to accept them, over and over again, if need be. While it doesn't feel good to receive half-hearted apologies, we can continue to offer the grace of forgiveness and trust that God is doing good work in the heart of the offender.

While we lovingly forgive others, God can lovingly change each of our hearts.

April 19

OWNING OUR ANGER

Control your temper, for anger labels you a fool.

ECCLESIASTES 7:9

Have you ever grown passionately angry with someone who, in that same moment, remained unspeakably calm? While your blood is boiling, heart is racing and body is shaking, they seem completely in control, breathing deeply and sitting coolly. Doesn't their peacefulness make you feel even madder?!

Our anger can easily take control of our words and actions – and, once it does, it takes much less effort to further ignite the anger than to extinguish it. Anger escalates quickly and soon speaks and behaves for us. To remain ourselves, even in the midst of feeling angry, is not easy, but deep breaths, long walks and a break from the anger-inducing circumstances can all help to keep us grounded, even in the fire of our anger.

If we were all able to remain in control, breathing deeply and sitting coolly, our anger could move towards productivity and healing rather than violence and foolishness.

April 20

CUTTING OUT COMPARISONS

*People are counted as righteous,
not because of their work, but because
of their faith in God who forgives sinners.*

ROMANS 4:5

Is there someone in your faith community who seems to do *all* the right things? She has the capacity to volunteer for several groups and events, *and* she does the work well. Maybe she can relate deeply to many or has giftedness seemingly matched by no other. In short, this woman is nearly saintly in her work. How can we ever compare to that?

Well, the good news is – we don't have to. Our gifts, capacities and callings are all different. The work we are doing is not being measured on some grand chart, marking our productivity in the kingdom of God. What matters most is the condition of our heart.

Are we loving God and others? Maybe we are communicating love through being on several committees – but maybe we're not. We need not compare our works to that of others, so let's take a deep breath and exhale God's love into our communities, in whatever way suits us best!

April 21

REJECTING REJECTION

*"Those the Father has given Me will
come to Me, and I will never reject them."*

JOHN 6:37

At some point in our lives, we all face some sort of rejection – and it is miserable. Few things feel more isolating, lonely and disorienting than being told that we are, essentially, not good enough. Whether it is in the context of a relationship, job or team, to be excluded is a reality that is difficult to find comfort in. What if we're good enough for a particular job or relationship *now*, but are pushed out in the future? That is an uncertainty that can potentially bring us unspeakable pain.

Our belonging, however, in the relationship we have with God is without uncertainty. It is a safe relationship, one without rejection. In fact, Jesus' rejection on earth, climaxing with His death on the cross, has saved us from an eternity of rejection. So if you are feeling outcast, isolated and lonely, take comfort in the eternal relationship we have with God, where our rejection is never an option.

April 22

FACT-CHECKING

*Do not spread slanderous
gossip among your people.*

LEVITICUS 19:16

These days, with text messaging, e-mail and social media, news spreads like wildfire. We have the potential of finding out about the happenings in our friend circles, nation and world within minutes of the event. What this also means, however, is that words can be shared that are not necessarily accurate.

With so much access to sharing information with great amounts of people also comes the responsibility of sharing credible, honest and fair information.

We can easily hide behind our cell phone or computer as we hit "send," releasing words about a person or event into the world for the public to see. We need to ensure that our character and integrity is in tact before each message we write is delivered – is the message true? Is it fair? Is it our story to tell?

Let's pause before we "send," and contribute honorable news to our communities.

April 23

PERSONAL INVENTORY

"Don't store up treasures here on earth,
where moths eat them and rust destroys them,
and where thieves break in and steal. Store your treasures in
heaven, where moths and rust cannot destroy, and thieves do not
break in and steal."

MATTHEW 6:19-20

Where do you keep all of your stuff? Do you have just enough to fill your home? Do you have a storage unit or a pile of belongings in the trunk of your car? As the years go by, it is so easy for our stuff to pile up, as we slowly add to it without taking much away from it.

Intentionality is greatly needed when considering all of our belongings. We need to be willing to ask ourselves what it is that we *actually* need, versus what we want. Our stuff can slowly begin to flood our lives, taking up more and more space for reasons we're unsure of. When we intentionally take stock of all we own and allow simplicity to enter the room, we may begin to breathe easier as our loads lighten.

After all, we cannot take any of our stuff with us at the end of our days!

April 24

EXERCISING OUR "NO" MUSCLE

God has given each of you a gift ...
Use them well to serve one another.

1 PETER 4:10

Do you ever find yourself burned out? You've been working too hard for too many consecutive days, going to bed late and waking up early. You're feeling over-committed and under-resourced, saying "yes" to so many events, projects and committees that you begin wondering if you simply forgot how to say the word "no!"

When we "crash," so to speak, from being so burnt out, we are not able to serve anyone, let alone ourselves. Having intensely busy seasons of life undoubtedly happens but, even still, we need to be wise in how we use our time, making space for rest and refreshment, lest we grow too exhausted to serve at all. If we continue pushing ourselves to use our gifts without pause, we may hit a wall, where our exhaustion will prevent us from using our gifts at all. Let's practice wisdom and discernment, even in the use of our gifts and service to others!

April 25

UP, DOWN AND ALL AROUND

*Jesus said, "I tell you the truth, unless you turn from your sins
and become like little children, you will never get into the
Kingdom of Heaven. So anyone who becomes as humble
as this little child is the greatest in the Kingdom of Heaven."*

MATTHEW 18:2-4

In our churches, jobs and schools, we are often "looking up" to the older people in the community. They have lived more years, wrestled with more questions and discovered more answers. We are, in many ways, following in the footsteps of the more seasoned ones walking before us. These people are good and helpful resources to look towards for advice and example.

What about, however, also "looking down" to the younger girls and boys in our community? What can we take from the example of a child? They haven't lived as many years, wrestled with as many questions or discovered as many answers. However, the beauty of a child's faith is that, oftentimes, they don't feel the need to wrestle with questions or search for answers. To have child-like faith means that we can trust in God's faithfulness without needing much more than the promise of His word, which has already been offered to us.

April 26

GENERATIVE FRIENDSHIPS

As iron sharpens iron, so a friend sharpens a friend.

PROVERBS 27:17

What are some of your favorite things to do with your friends? Do you go shopping, see movies or cook with one another? It is a great blessing in life to have friends who we can have fun, laughter-filled, light-hearted experiences with. What a gift!

Friendships, however, are not *only* for fun and laughter (although they are *great* for offering us those things!). Our friendships will, hopefully, provide a safe environment for each person's refinement. When we trust and respect our friends, we have, in those relationships, people who we can both teach and learn from. Our friendships should be a place where we can admit fault, receive grace and be corrected in love. We should definitely be enjoying our time with friends, but we should also allow those relationships to go deeper, to a place where grace and refinement live freely.

How are you offering and receiving loving re-finement in your friendships?

April 27

WHAT'S IN A NAME?

The LORD called me before my birth; from within the womb He called me by name.

ISAIAH 49:1

Is there a particular version of your name you hear when you know you've screwed up, or when you're being addressed by people who don't know you? Our names are one of our primary identifying factors – they help to set us apart from others. When people know our name, they know more of us; they can identify us and call us out. When our names are known, more of who we are is known.

In our earliest moments on this earth, we were named. Since then, we have been identified and addressed by that name. We have, to some degree, been known. But, even before our cries were heard on this earth, our Heavenly Father identified us. He knew us intimately; He called us by name. Our name is not *all* of who we are, but it is a part of us. May we embrace our name – we are identified; we are known!

April 28

GIVING LOVE, LOVE GIVING

If someone has enough money to live well
and sees a brother or sister in need but shows no
compassion – how can God's love be in that person?

1 JOHN 3:17

There is certainly no shortage of opportunities to give and, oftentimes, we can feel somewhat bombarded with the needs that are so pronounced all around us. We are directed to be as generous as we can, so the instructions here are clear. How, though, do we behave when we are giving?

It is good, kind and godly to be generous with our belongings in order to meet the needs of others. Is the kindness and godliness still there, however, when we give begrudgingly? Is it an act of love when we give some of our resources to a person in need, but do so with a cold heart and irritated attitude? Generosity is a loving act, but it can be done without much love. Let us focus on giving willingly and joyously, considering it an honor to have the resources to bless others!

April 29

A HOLY ATTACHMENT

"Be sure of this: I am with you
always, even to the end of the age."

MATTHEW 28:20

Have you ever seen a parent and young child in public, attached to one another by some sort of bracelet, so as to prevent the child from getting lost? It is actually like a leash, of sorts, but prevents the child from wandering too far away from his or her parent. This, then, reassures both the child and the caretaker that they will not be separated, even when navigating their way through a crowd.

As we are journeying through life, that sort of attachment is available with God. He will (and wants to!) remain connected to us through the various seasons and crowds we find ourselves in.

He offers to remain close to us, so we will not wander or become lost. His nearness, even in times of wandering or trouble, is a promise He makes to us. He will be with us, attached to us, ensuring our safety.

April 30

May

POLITELY DIVINE

Come close to God, and God will come close to you.

James 4:8

God is not intrusive. He will not force Himself into our lives, regardless of our desire. He'll call to us and always answer when we call, but He will not disregard our desires. If we don't want Him to be near us, He may very well soften His step around us.

But what about when we call Him to come near? No matter how close or far we've kept Him in the past, He'll move toward us without hesitation. God does not play games with us – when we seek Him, we will find Him seeking us. Even if we kept our distance from God yesterday (or for hundreds of "yesterdays"), when we cry out, He is there. He is not meddlesome, but He certainly is available!

What sweet relief it is to know that no matter how often we draw close, and then run away, God will remain steadily available to us!

DIVINE ANSWERS

"When you are arrested, don't worry
about how to respond or what to say. God
will give you the right words at the right time."

MATTHEW 10:19

It can be difficult to discuss our faith in God with other people, particularly those who don't share our faith, because having faith does not equate to having all of the answers. We don't necessarily have proof – we have faith. It can be hard or scary to explain that to others.

However, God is big enough and powerful enough to speak *through* us, rather than sit back and watch us fumbling for words. When we find ourselves in need of His help, ask Him, and believe He can give you the words to speak. As well, He could give the listener ears to hear and understand you in a way that they may not normally have been able.

We are not solely responsible for talking about our faith. God is with us in that, too, and can boldly present Himself in difficult conversations. Your words need not be your own!

May 2

BLIND ENCOUNTERS

*"Look beneath the surface
so you can judge correctly."*

JOHN 7:24

What is it like to first speak to someone on the phone or via email before meeting them in person? How is that first meeting different because you already have an idea of what their voice sounds like or how it feels to be in written communication with them? Are your initial thoughts, upon seeing them, different than they would be if you didn't have an existing relationship?

Our opinions about others can be quite potent, and that which we see with our eyes often speaks louder than the ways we experience a person's character, particularly during initial meetings.

How can we quiet the judgments our eyes make so that we can have the space to get to know and experience one's character? May we let their heart speak louder than our vision!

May 3

THE "I DO" OF A LIFETIME

The LORD made this covenant with you so that no man, woman, family, or tribe among you would turn away from the LORD to worship these gods of other nations, and so that no root among you would bear bitter and poisonous fruit.

DEUTERONOMY 29:18

One of the sweetest parts of attending a wedding is to hear the couple say aloud the promises they are making to one another for a lifetime of fidelity, commitment and honor.

Whether or not we get married, we can be involved in similar vows. God has promised us His faithfulness, presence and grace – and we can do the same. Much like a marriage, we are not to honor other gods before our God; we are to spend time with Him, treat Him with honor and be honest with Him. The commitments we make with God are like the ultimate vows; as they are made (and kept!), we not only receive a lifetime with this One, we receive the promise of an *eternity* with Him!

Would you add anything to the vows you make to God? What part is most challenging for you? Even in the difficulties of this promise, you can talk to Him about it!

May 4

LISTEN UP, WORLD!

I am not ashamed of this Good News about
Christ. It is the power of God at work, saving
everyone who believes – the Jew first and also the Gentile.

ROMANS 1:16

Have you ever been so excited about something that you could hardly contain your enthusiasm? Maybe you were offered the job you wanted, entered a loving relationship or won a free tropical vacation! These are all such good things that we want to share with others! You could literally shout it from the rooftops – or share the news on social media, call your friends or even throw a party to celebrate!

When we acknowledge God's love, grace and presence in our lives, the reality of it is so great that we might actually be bursting to share about it! He takes such delight in seeing our enthusiasm about His love, and desires that we not hesitate to share that enthusiasm with others. We have been saved by grace and get an eternity with our Savior in heaven – that definitely sounds like something to shout about from the rooftops!

May 5

ETERNAL INVESTMENT

If we are unfaithful, He remains
faithful, for He cannot deny who He is.

2 TIMOTHY 2:13

Well, if you're going to break the rules, then SO AM I!

Do you ever feel justified in doing less than you are capable of just because the person you are in a relationship or working with isn't doing their best? It certainly feels easier to lower our effort when those around us are. It is hard to remain as invested or committed to something when those we were invested *with* have lost interest or motivation.

Our integrity, however, can be stronger than the challenge or disappointment of another's hurtful disinterest. To remain steadfast in our commitments, regardless of what others are doing, reveals godliness in character.

When considering our relationship with God, we can be certain that His effort, level of commitment and interest in us will never waver. He remains solid; still available when we may waver, but never growing disinterested in a relationship with us.

May 6

HEAVEN AWAITS

"God blesses those who are poor and realize their need for Him, for the Kingdom of Heaven is theirs."

MATTHEW 5:3

Being included in someone's will is most definitely an honor; this act communicates that they see us as one who has invested in them, and they want to bless us, even after they have passed away. To be in a person's will most often indicates that there was a relationship – and a meaningful one, at that.

When we enter into relationship with God, we are added to His will, so to speak. He wants to bless us for committing to Him, and so He adds us as one who receives the eternal gift of life.

We cannot, however, receive this blessing without a relationship with Him, just as we would not be included in the will of a complete stranger.

God sees and honors the investment we make in our relationship with Him – there is no greater return for our investment than eternal life!

SPEAK UP!

*Everyone who calls on the
name of the LORD will be saved.*

ACTS 2:21

Have you ever found yourself desperately need-ing something, but you didn't speak up and ask for it? Did you get what you needed? Maybe you were too shy, ashamed or afraid. Maybe you weren't sure who to ask, or how to ask.

We all need saving. As sinful beings, we cannot receive the gift of eternal life without acknowledging our need for God to save us from our sins. How can we receive God's grace and salvation without asking Him for it – without telling Him we know we need it! He will not push it on us, but will hear us when we speak our needs to Him.

Have you allowed timidity, shame or fear to keep you from asking for God's salvation? Call on Him, as often as you need, and He'll answer you!

May 8

WEAK FEAR, STRONG GOD

Jesus responded, "Why are you afraid? You have so
little faith!" Then He got up and rebuked the wind
and waves, and suddenly there was a great calm.

MATTHEW 8:26

Think back to some of your darkest days. Maybe difficult times are a distant memory, or maybe they are your current reality. Either way, let's wonder about the scary, anxiety-inducing, grim moments of our lives and think: what is it that we were afraid of? What, in any given situation that comes to mind, was the origin of your fear – death, illness, poverty, abandonment? Are any of your causes for fear bigger than God?

It is natural to experience fear, but we really don't have to! God's saving grace is real, available and larger than life! His care overpowers whatever earthly things may try to destruct us. Even if life is taken from us here on earth, life is given to us eternally with God.

We do not need to exhaust ourselves on fearfulness, because it is no match for God's protection and grace!

May 9

IN TIME

God says, "At just the right time, I heard you.
On the day of salvation, I helped you." Indeed,
the "right time" is now. Today is the day of salvation.

2 CORINTHIANS 6:2

Timing, some would say, is everything. It is frustrating when what we're looking for shows up *after* we need it. That seems to happen all too often, doesn't it?

We may often feel like we cannot trust that our needs will be met in a timely manner, but we can trust that God is aware of our needs and our desired timetable. That does not mean that He will show up and reveal Himself in the ways that we ask, when we ask, but we can trust that His timing is a bit more impeccable than our own. We do not hold the fullest picture of our lives. God is better suited at deciding what the right place at the right time actually means for us – all we need to do is trust His judgment.

Timing might feel like it is "everything," but the timing is not always our own!

HOLDING GRUDGES HOLDS US BACK

Love does not demand its own way. It is not irritable, and it keeps no record of being wronged.

1 CORINTHIANS 13:5

Holding grudges against another is like putting both of you in an inescapable prison. We may proclaim, "I forgive you!" after being wronged, but when we continue to resurface the offense, we are holding the offender *and* ourselves in the pain of the wrong-doing.

When our loved one hurts us (and they will), the love we feel for them is bigger than the grudge we're tempted to hold. Grudges make it impossible for anyone involved in a hurtful circumstance to experience the real freedom of forgiveness. Is there a time when a loved one hurt you that you still remind them of? What is gained by continuing to remind someone of how they have hurt us?

Let's allow love to release us from the hold our grudges have on our relationships!

May 11

EVERYDAY "CHORES"

*Let's not get tired of doing what is
good. At just the right time we will reap
a harvest of blessing if we don't give up.*

GALATIANS 6:9

Did your parents ever give you a list of chores to do when you were younger? If you completed your chores, then you could watch TV or go outside and play; you were done with your responsibilities for the day!

Now, do you ever feel that way with serving others? Maybe you called to check in on a friend, brought coffee for a co-worker, tipped a nice waiter a little extra and volunteered your time in the community. Whew! It's hard not to think, "I've done my good deeds for the day!" and then simply collapse, inwardly focused, until the next day of doing good is upon us.

Here's the thing: the days of good deeds is the life we are called to live! We should not approach service to others as chores to be completed, but as a joy-filled aspect of serving God. The reward to be gained is far greater than an hour of TV!

May 12

HELP & HEALING

*Putting confidence in an unreliable
person is like chewing with a broken
tooth or walking on a lame foot.*

PROVERBS 25:19

People make mistakes. This is a reality that we've been hearing and experiencing for most of our lives. There are, however, different kinds of mistakes. Awareness plays a significant role in the nature of our missteps. Are we conscious of our poor judgment, or are we simply unaware of the negative impact of our actions, therefore keeping us from repentance?

There will always be room for us to grow in our awareness, but we can learn from what we do know. It would be foolish to continue walking on a broken foot, without seeking help or healing for our ailing body.

Similarly, we would be undiscerning to continue choosing to live in sin. When something does not feel right, wise, or godly, we should pause to seek help and healing!

May 13

INESCAPABLE TOLLS

Jesus told him, "I am the way, the truth, and the life.
No one can come to the Father except through Me."

JOHN 14:6

Paying tolls is a pretty inescapable reality for many travelers these days. If we do not have enough money to pay the toll, then we might be stuck – the gate will remain in front of us, preventing us from moving forward; or, a bill is sent to us in the mail, demanding we pay the cost of the unpaid toll.

The price of following God is different, though accepting Jesus as our Savior is, in a similar fashion, an inescapable reality that we need to acknowledge if we'd like to continue walking with God.

If we do not find our salvation in Jesus, then we won't get very far – we won't move forward or we'll somehow slip by.

Are we trying to outrun our giver of life, or have we acknowledged our need for Him today?

May 14

CARRY ME

*"Come to Me, all of you who are weary and
carry heavy burdens, and I will give you rest."*

MATTHEW 11:38

Do you remember, in younger years, staying up a bit too late and your parent or caretaker carrying your sleepy, nearly limp body to bed? It always felt like such a relief! "Phew, I don't have to get out of the car or off the couch and walk to bed; Dad is doing the work for me!"

As adults, we don't really have that luxury anymore. Regardless of how exhausted we feel, we must stand up and walk ourselves to bed (or to work, to school, to a meeting, etc.). Our exhaustion in adulthood may be deeper than in childhood, but our resources often feel fewer.

God may not literally carry us to bed, but He is the most valuable resource we could have. When we share our exhaustion or worries with Him, He carries them for us, lightening the load, so we have more energy to take our weary selves to bed.

May 15

"ONE" MATTERS

"There is joy in the presence of God's
angels when even one sinner repents."

LUKE 15:10

One goal scored, one dollar made, one pound lost. "One" can be a pretty discouraging number, especially in a world where bigger is usually better. God, however, has a different perspective. He doesn't just count what *should* or *could* be, but celebrates what *is*!

Did you score one goal, make one dollar or lose one pound? That's "one" more (or less, in some cases!) than you once had! Woohoo! Let's give ourselves permission to celebrate that which seems small, because it is the small things that lead to the big things. One person coming to God is one more who will know His goodness and grace – and that's reason to celebrate!

The small and singular still matter in big ways! What little things deserve acknowledgement and celebration today?

May 16

ACCESSIBLE GIFTS

*Since we know He hears us when
we make our requests, we also know
that He will give us what we ask for.*

1 JOHN 5:15

Online shopping – it's simple, accessible and convenient! With a few clicks of a button, we can order nearly anything from nearly anywhere in the world and receive it at our doorstep in just a number of days. What is it that you want? Think of something ordinary or absurd – chances are, it's available online and you can purchase and receive it without ever leaving your couch.

What about the intangible things – the ones that are much more significant than owning a shoe organizer for our closet or a 60-piece container set for the kitchen. We can order an innumerable amount of things online, but we won't find God's grace, deep peace or authentic joy for sale on the Internet. It is, however, just as simple, accessible and convenient to receive. We don't need to leave our couch or even have Internet access. What does your soul need and desire? Speak it out to God – He'll deliver!

May 17

INTENTIONAL INVITES

*Then [Jesus] turned to His host. "When you put on a luncheon
or a banquet," He said, "don't invite your friends, brothers,
relatives, and rich neighbors. Instead, invite the poor, the crippled,
the lame, and the blind. Then at the resurrection of the righteous,
God will reward you for inviting those who could not repay you."*

LUKE 14:12-14

Do you have a particular group of friends that you enjoy spending most of your free time with? Maybe you've spent enough hours with them that hanging out together is just so easy – you know who will bring what to dinner, the conversation flows effortlessly and the jokes are understood by everyone.

It is good to have a close group of friends to connect with, but what happens to our fellowship and hospitality when we're consistently hosting the same people? We unintentionally shut down our pursuit of other people, along with our opportunity to expand our "hospitality reach."

Belonging to a particular community is a rich blessing, but let's remain intentional about inviting others into our lives and our homes, as well. Our invitation might be an unspeakable blessing for lonely people!

May 18

SELF-CONTROL MATTERS

Knowing God leads to self-control,
self-control leads to patient endurance,
and patient endurance leads to godliness.

2 PETER 1:6

What is the point of self-control!? I mean, is it really such a big deal? If I lose control of myself for one night, for the sake of a party or a romantic evening with my boyfriend, who is really going to know? Even if a few people know, who is actually going to care? Is it really so important that we maintain our self-control – and why?

Self-control matters to God and, therefore, should matter to us. If we indulge in an activity that we shouldn't, even if in private, God knows. In addition to His awareness of our indulgence, we are pulled farther away from living in His image. Maintaining self-control is what helps our lives reflect godliness. Maintaining control of what we speak out, put in our body, or do with our body cultivates a godly character within us – a way of being that can positively impact others!

THE JEALOUS FIGHT

*A peaceful heart leads to a healthy
body; jealousy is like cancer in the bones.*

PROVERBS 14:30

What do you see when you observe the life of another? Do you notice a nicer car, bigger home or thinner body? Does she seem to have more stylish clothes, a happier home life, or closer friendships? What happens in our own selves when we experience jealousy? Our jaw may tighten, our stomach ties up in knots or our face gets hot. None of this feels very pleasant!

Jealousy is a powerful emotion that actually physically manifests itself in various ways in our body. Not only does jealousy impact our relationships, but it can impact our own physical well-being too. What levels of peace and wellness in our own lives are being replaced by jealousy? How many hours of our lives are being eaten up by envy? Let's take a deep breath and fight back when jealousy threatens to take away our peace.

Counting our own blessings could be a great place to start!

May 20

COME CLOSER, SWEET HOPE

*All glory to God, who is able, through His
mighty power at work within us, to accomplish
infinitely more than we might ask or think.*

EPHESIANS 3:20

We are all in dire need of saving. Though our days may include laughter, joy and celebration, there is also no shortage of sorrow and pain in our world. People are being senselessly killed, brutally raped and violently beaten. We need not travel far to meet those who are homeless, voiceless or both. Chaos is literally erupting in our streets and, oftentimes, one glance at the headlines is all it takes to feel overwhelmed with hopelessness.

I know God can save, but can He save all of THIS?

He really can. It's difficult to hold on to hope when hope feels so far away, but God can save us, *and them.* Of course we feel overwhelmed when we take an honest look at our world – because it is too much for us to handle. But, God can. God will. Lord, save us; bring unthinkable amounts of peace to Your people.

May 21

WHEN DISTINCTIONS FADE

All who have been united with Christ in baptism
have put on Christ, like putting on new clothes.
There is no longer Jew or Gentile, slave or free,
male and female. For you are all one in Christ Jesus.

GALATIANS 3:27-28

How do you distinguish yourself from another? What sort of differences do you name? Are they physical – your hair, height, skin color, sex or weight? What about your job, level of education, place of residence or relationship status? We can notice differences in our family of origin, hobbies or giftedness too. In fact, the distinctions we can make between another and ourselves are nearly endless! We are unique individuals!

Our individuality is to be celebrated, but there is something that brings us all together, blurring the lines of distinction between each person. Our belonging to Christ unifies us more than our distinctions separate us. While God created and loves our individuality, we can join Him in also seeing each person as a child of God, rather than the label that their appearance or successes offer them. How does it change things to see others first as God's beloved?

May 22

SHARING IN GRIEF

*"God blesses those who mourn,
for they will be comforted."*

MATTHEW 5:4

How do you communicate to others when you are hurting? Do you tell them, weep in their presence, or get quiet and hope that they can guess when you are not doing well? It is incredibly vulnerable to admit when we're scared or hurting. However, it is in this admittance when others then know that we need help, comfort and grace. When we hide our grief, we're also blocking others from meeting us in our places of deep sadness.

There are many things to be mourned in our broken world. When we cry out in our grief, we are not only vulnerably and authentically expressing our emotions, but we're also asking for comfort – for some sort of relief from the pain.

When we mourn, we are inviting God (and sometimes others, too) into our grief, communicating that we don't want to go about it alone.

MANY SIDES, ONE STORY

*Intelligent people are always ready to
learn. Their ears are open for knowledge.*

PROVERBS 18:15

There are two sides to every story. This reminder is often offered to young ones who are judging, fighting or gossiping with one another. These days, however, with our increased accessibility to news and information, there are often countless sides to every story.

So many people have differing opinions on the same topic, many of which are shared on TV, blogs or social media, that it can be disorienting to try and form our own opinion.

What's important is not to get overwhelmed by the sheer volume of the information around us, but to recognize that it is around us. We should never become stagnant in our learning. Whether the topic is our faith or what sort of diet prevents cancer, having an open mind and recognizing that we don't have all of the answers is what will help to keep us on the path of growth!

May 24

SELECTIVE HEARING

"No one can serve two masters.
For you will hate one and love the other;
you will be devoted to one and despise the
other. You cannot serve both God and money."

LUKE 16:13

Have you ever only selectively followed your boss's instructions at work? You listen to her directions for some things, but follow self-instructions with other things. All day, you go back and forth, obeying her and then yourself, her and then you.

While there may be room for your own ideas, you cannot honor your boss's position and authority when you consistently choose to follow your own instruction. A dedicated and valuable employee may offer her own suggestions, but will listen attentively to the directions her boss sets. We cannot select which instructions we follow.

In the same way, we must honor God's authority in our life, above all other beings and things. When we obey Him sometimes, following the instruction or values of another at other times, we're not really following Him. His word and authority should be honored above all else!

May 25

A FOOLPROOF PLAN

The LORD is good, a strong refuge when trouble comes. He is close to those who trust in Him.

NAHUM 1:7

Where is it that you are to go if a tornado or hurricane is headed your way? Safety precautions in natural disasters are often similar, depending on the circumstance. We know that a windowless basement will probably keep us the safest if a tornado touches down near us, so we make that our place of refuge. We are not, however, guaranteed safety and wellness just because we are in the basement. Isn't that maddening? We might take all of the necessary precautions, and still be unable to escape harm.

Our eternal refuge in Christ is far more dependable than any basement or windowless shelter. When we escape to Him, we are met with guaranteed safety in the midst of any difficulty or danger. God promises to take care of us, to be near us and to save us from death. He is our most dependable refuge in the face of any disaster.

May 26

DREAM ON

Hope deferred makes the heart sick,
but a dream fulfilled is a tree of life.

PROVERBS 13:12

What is it that your heart desires? Are you aching to be a wife, a mom, a teacher or an actress? What dreams are alive within you, even if they're covered with layers of doubt and fear?

How does our discouragement and unbelief dull our dreams until we can hardly acknowledge them, let alone hope and pray that they become our reality?

Our dreams and aspirations are a part of us; many of them are instilled in us by God, Himself! It is a sad form of surrender when we choose to stop pursuing our dreams because of hopelessness or despair. They may not all come true at the same time or in the way we imagine them to, but simply foregoing our dreams is far more painful than dreaming and waiting!

UNDER THE MICROSCOPE

When you say they are wicked and should be punished, you are condemning yourself, for you who judge others do these very same things.

ROMANS 2:1

Celebrities are scrutinized by particularly watchful eyes these days. Not only are many public figures unable to go out for lunch or to the grocery store without being photographed, but they are often held to a nearly impossible standard. Sure, as celebrities, they should be setting a sound example for the rest of society, but are we holding ourselves to a similar standard?

It's easy for us to read a story about an actress or a politicians' misstep and condemn them, either in our thoughts or our words. What, however, would others say about us – should our lives be under the microscope, so to speak? When we speak of another's wrongdoing, are we trying to turn attention away from our own sin?

Before we indulge in hearing of a celebrity's poor judgment, let's consider our own need for refinement.

May 28

NOTICE AND BE NOTICED

*"Everyone who acknowledges
Me publicly here on earth, I will also
acknowledge before My Father in heaven."*

MATTHEW 10:32

Have you ever seen someone at the grocery store who you didn't want to talk to? Did you make a run for it, attempting to hide in the cereal aisle, then checking every aisle before walking down it, to ensure it was "safe?"

We can convince ourselves that conversing with that individual would involve too much time, drama or fake laughter. Maybe they're always seeking us out to join a committee or attend a social event. Whatever the case, how painful would it be if we were the one being avoided at all costs?

The same is true in our relationship with God. We may have days when we don't acknowledge Him or admit our relationship with Him to others. Maybe it would involve too much time or commitment to do so. Whatever the case, our avoidance of Him is deeply painful to Him. Call Him by name and He'll call your name!

GRASPING THE UNGRASPABLE

May you have the power to understand,
as all God's people should, how wide, how
long, how high, and how deep His love is.

EPHESIANS 3:18

Can you grasp how deep the ocean is, how high the sky is or how many stars speckle our universe? There are things in this world that our minds simply cannot fully comprehend. Of all of those things, however, God's love for us should be among the most potent.

How many different creatures or colors exist in creation? We might think we know, but we cannot be certain! We might think we can put into words how deeply God loves us, but it's probably an inch more than *that* (and then another inch more than *that*, and a foot deeper than *that*). To comprehend God's love for each of us may mean that we admit how unfathomable something so vast, deep, and rich really is.

Can you say how wide, long, high and deep God loves you? Because I bet it's a bit wider than that – and a bit longer, higher and deeper, too.

May 30

MINDFUL OF OUR MINDS

They promise freedom, but they
themselves are slaves of sin and corruption.
For you are a slave to whatever controls you.

2 PETER 2:19

What is it that takes up the most space in your mind? Do you worry about money, wonder about your appearance or analyze the happenings in your relationships? Are you consistently thinking about food, working out, or the TV show that you just can't get enough of?

It can be so easy for these things to infiltrate our thoughts until suddenly we find that thoughts of anything eternal are drowned out by our fixations on the worldly. Are we being Christ followers when we're only thinking about Christ on Sunday mornings? To truly give our lives to Him means that we release the hold that worldly things have on us. Of course, this does not mean we should never think about our relationships or our finances, but when this is what we're most often thinking about, we are (consciously or not) being controlled by it. What's on your mind today?!

May 31

June

NO NEWS IS GOOD NEWS

As surely as a north wind brings rain,
so a gossiping tongue causes anger!

PROVERBS 25:23

What are our motivations for gossiping? We might convince ourselves that we're actually offering a service, of sorts, in sharing news and information with others. That certainly would help us feel confirmed in our decision to speak about others to others! In truth, however, we are serving no one but ourselves.

The news and information being spread in gossip is not ours to share, but we could easily feel empowered by the influence or popularity we feel when we have gossip to spread.

Our acclaim, however, is only fleeting until the next round of gossip comes in; and, in the meantime, we've deeply dishonored the ones whom we're gossiping about.

In the end, we've served no one by spreading words about others – not even ourselves.

June 1

WISH LISTS

*You want what you don't have, so you scheme
and kill to get it. You are jealous of what others
have, but you can't get it, so you fight and wage
war to take it away from them. Yet you don't have
what you want because you don't ask God for it.*

JAMES 4:2

Have you ever had a friend who was incredibly verbal about something she wanted? Be it a particular handbag, book, or techy gadget, she would *not* tire of expressing her desire. So, is anybody *really* surprised when she ends up receiving it? Of course not! When a person so openly expresses their desire for something, it's not unthinkable that somebody in their life would do what they can to fulfill it.

Maybe we respond by calling her spoiled or exclaiming, "She ALWAYS gets what she wants!" Doesn't it help, however, that she asks for what she wants? What desires of ours are we keeping quiet, while simultaneously feeling frustrated that we haven't received what we want? Can we slowly begin to voice our desires, both to God and our loved ones? It's a vulnerable task, but the fruit of our risk may be just what we're wanting!

June 2

BEAUTY IN THE BLISTERS

*How beautiful on the mountains are
the feet of the messenger who brings
good news, the good news of peace and
salvation, the news that the God of Israel reigns!*

ISAIAH 52:7

It is a luxury to receive a pedicure. Oftentimes, customers will sit in big, comfortable chairs with built-in massage capabilities while the employees pamper their feet and legs. By the end of the occasion, the pedicure recipient has clean, soft feet and flawlessly colorful toes. What a treat!

To God, though, post-pedicure feet are not the most beautiful feet He can imagine. As children of God, it is more about where our feet are taking us and the messages they're helping us to deliver than the delicacy or flawlessness of their appearance. It's fun to have bright pink polish on our toes, but it puts a sweet dent in eternity when our feet carry us to love others, tell people about Jesus and serve selflessly.

Are your feet calloused, blistered and dirty? Did they carry you to love another well today? Well, then – how radiant they are!

June 3

SLIPPING, SLIDING, REACHING

When you go through deep waters, I will be with you.

ISAIAH 43:2

What do you do when you find yourself slipping or falling? For many, our immediate reaction is to reach out our hand to grab someone or something around us – anything that can help to stabilize us as we lose control.

When things in our lives seem to be spinning out of control, what do you reach out your hand towards? Some of us may automatically reach for the remote control in an attempt to drown out the scariness of our lack of control. Some may reach for an alcoholic beverage, an unhealthy relationship or a buffet line. Whether we realize it or not, we're reaching for something when we're in trouble.

To avoid falling again right away, why don't we look towards a trusted friend, Scripture and God's presence? We will meet great trouble in our lives, but we can reach for solid resources to help us traverse the difficult waters.

June 4

Mallory Larsen

IN THE NAME OF LOVE

*You must love the LORD your God with all
your heart, all your soul, and all your strength.*

DEUTERONOMY 6:5

Have you ever been in love? He's the last person you think about before you go to sleep and the first one on your mind the next morning. You regularly wonder about ways that you can serve him, meet his needs and enrich his quality of life. You would make sacrifices and do things you wouldn't normally do, all in the name of love!

Imagine how it could change our mood, and the trajectory of our day, if God was the One we thought about before we fell asleep and immediately upon waking up. What sorts of things would we be led to do if we were fixated on serving Him, making sacrifices for Him and doing things we wouldn't normally do, all in the name of our love for Him!

We would probably end up spreading love to a whole lot of people as we grow more and more in the image of our greatest Love!

HUMILITY CHECK

"Those who exalt themselves will be humbled,
and those who humble themselves will be exalted."

LUKE 14:11

Don't you love leaving the house wearing a brand-new ensemble? Maybe we're rocking a great pair of high heels, perfect-fitting jeans and a blouse that catches glances. As the day goes on, we might grow increasingly aware of how many people are noticing how fabulous we look. What a great feeling! With every compliment and glance, our head inflates, even slightly. Before we know it, we may not be even concerned with what people know about us, because it feels so good to be noticed for how attractive we are!

This is pride and God despises pride. In these moments, we could use a figurative face-plant as we're strutting down the street, in order to bring us back to a level of humility. God delights in our delight of ourselves, but when humble delight turns into deep pride, where we're feeding off of compliments and glances, then it's time for a serious humility check.

LABOR PAINS

Dear friends, don't be surprised at the fiery trials you are going through, as if something strange were happening to you. Instead, be very glad – for these trials make you partners with Christ in His suffering, so that you will have the wonderful joy of seeing His glory when it is revealed to all the world.

1 PETER 4:12-13

Whether or not you have experienced it yourself, it is no secret that the pregnancy and birthing process can be one of the most intensely painful processes that a human being can experience. Though it is different for every woman, there's no denying that birthing a child is not done without some pain. Bringing life into this world is a delicate and laborious process.

But after the pain of labor, a new life is in our arms! It is a miracle beyond comprehension, and though the process can be tumultuous, how worthwhile it is when that baby's skin touches our own.

The process of walking with God, committing to and sacrificing for Him, will not always be easy. We may endure rejection, temptation and attacks by the evil one, but nothing will be as worthwhile as a heavenly eternity with God. Through the pain, glory will come.

STAYIN' ALIVE

If we love each other, God lives in us, and
His love is brought to full expression in us.

1 JOHN 4:12

How do you keep the memory alive of a loved one who has passed away? We may bring them up in conversation, put photos of them around our home or listen to their favorite music.

Each time we intentionally revive their memory in our lives, we are honoring who they were (and still are!) to us.

In the same way, each time we love another from a place of selflessness in our heart, we are honoring God and keeping the memory of Him alive.

There is no better way to remember Him, who He was, and who He very much still is, than loving people as He does. It's His favorite tune to hear and sight to see; and it is how we can keep Him alive within us and through us.

FLAT-OUT, MERCY-FILLED

When God our Savior revealed His kindness
and love, He saved us, not because of the
righteous things we had done, but because
of His mercy. He washed away our sins.

TITUS 3:4-5

Imagine being stranded on the side of the road, a tire of your car flat as a pancake. You're not particularly well trained in changing a tire, and could use a helping hand (or two). You are alone, far from home and without cell phone service. These are dire circumstances.

As cars drive by the sad scene, what sort of credibility can you advertise about yourself that will get them to stop? In this case, you cannot depend on your own goodness being the reasons others stop to help. When someone stops, it will not be because they know you have earned their assistance through your actions; it will be because they believe that you, whoever you are, are worthy of being helped when in trouble. In a similar fashion, God comes to save us not because our deeds have earned his help, but because His love and grace need not pause to take account of our deeds.

June 9

GETTING BURNED

"Anyone who hears My teaching and doesn't obey it is foolish, like a person who builds a house on sand."

MATTHEW 7:26

Do you remember your mom telling you not to touch the stove, iron or casserole dish because "it's VERY hot!"? Were you all the more tempted to touch it, just to discover if she was right, or to see for yourself just *how* hot it was? We all know what happens next – if you touch the hot stove, you're going to get burned! Why not just listen to (and trust) her instructions in the first place?

It's so curious, when we're given directions for protection, yet we still choose to do otherwise, oftentimes leading us to pain, trouble or both. The same is true in our relationship with God. He offers us instructions, not only in the Bible, but also through teachings we hear and personal encounters we experience. Do we test boundaries or disobey in order to find out whether or not the teachings are trustworthy? If we listen and obey, we're less likely to get burned!

June 10

UNDISGUISED LOVE

Don't forget to show hospitality to strangers, for some who have done this have entertained angels without realizing it!

HEBREWS 13:2

Sometimes, a drastic haircut, weight loss or makeup application is all it takes for us to see a friend of ours without recognizing her. They may walk past us in the grocery store or even say hello at the coffee shop. What if we, in turn, walk right by her or even give her the cold shoulder?

Every person we come in contact with should be treated with the same respect we offer our friends and loved ones; and not only because they may actually *be* our friend or loved one! We can never be certain who is in our midst, be it a celebrity, unrecognizable loved one or a child of God who is simply lonely.

Let's set our baseline as treating everyone with respect, and then we can be pleasantly surprised at who those people may reveal themselves to be!

June 11

THE BEATEN PATH

Do not be afraid or discouraged, for the
LORD will personally go ahead of you. He will be
with you; He will neither fail you nor abandon you.

DEUTERONOMY 31:8

"I'll go ahead and scope out the scene, then come
back here and tell you what it's like!"

A phrase akin to this is like music to our ears! Whether our investigative pal is going to check out a car we want to purchase, restaurant we'd like to try or hike we'd like to take, it eases our anxiety to have someone go before us. Our pioneer, then, can offer us warnings, thoughtful advice and things to look for, try, or do. Bad surprises, fear and stress can be avoided when someone first travels the path before us!

What is causing you fear or stress? There are enough opportunities for us to face bad surprises these days, but can we remember that God has gone before us? He scopes out the scenes we're headed towards, offers us warnings and advice, and goes with us as we continue the journey. He's already been to the places you need to go!

June 12

A LIFELONG APPOINTMENT

*I am certain that God, who began the good
work within you, will continue His work until it is
finally finished on the day when Christ Jesus returns.*

PHILIPPIANS 1:6

Would you ever leave the salon with only one part of your head colored, or walk out of the dentist with half of your teeth cleaned? Of course not! We wait patiently until the hair stylist or dentist has completed their task, and then we go about our day. It would be unnatural, and probably end up requiring more effort to leave before the job is done!

God is continuing to refine our hearts, shape our character and renew our minds. Rather than running out the door before the task is completed, let us be patient and anticipate the inner beauty that is being cultivated within us.

We can continue to go about our day, but we need to give Him space to do His work in us!

GROWING JOY

The tongue can bring death or life; those
who love to talk will reap the consequences.

PROVERBS 18:21

There are two spray bottles that look exactly alike, both filled with a clear liquid. Spray either of them on your plants and flowers, and you will see a completely different result. One bottle is filled with water, the other with a plant killer. Who would have known?! The two are nearly indistinguishable, yet one gives life to the plants and the other takes it away.

Our words can be just as lethal or life-giving. Similar language used in different contexts or for differing purposes can produce wildly different results. Our words, however few or many we speak, have impact. We hold power to cultivate joy or smother confidence in the life of another.

Consider every sentence spoken to be like a spray from one of two bottles – let's speak life into others!

June 14

THE SAFEST BET

Love does no wrong to others.

ROMANS 13:10

Sometimes, in our churches, schools and workplaces, we tend to overcomplicate things. There are particular rules, socially acceptable norms and systems of belief that often vary between communities or individuals. Do you ever feel like it's too much to keep straight?

Here's a hint: loving another person is never a bad decision to make. When we find ourselves overwhelmed with various doctrines, rules and expectations, one core truth to remember is that treating someone with love will not cause harm, pain or regret. If we visit a sick friend, buy a meal for someone who is hungry or give our time to helping an exhausted co-worker, we are following a simple but tremendous instruction from God to love other people.

No matter how confused, disoriented or unsure we are of the teachings and guidelines around us, we cannot go wrong if we offer love to those in our midst.

PASSIONATE JOURNEY

"I know the plans I have for you," says the
LORD. "They are plans for good and not for
disaster, to give you a future and a hope."

Have you always known what you wanted to do with your life? Did you grow up pretending to be a teacher, artist or doctor, remaining tied to that desire as the years passed? That would certainly simplify things; but what about those of us whose minds and plans change? What if the aspirations we held when we were younger are ones we evolve out of?

It is often frustrating to be met with confusion or disorientation around what we should be doing with our lives.

What drives us when we can't find our burning passion in life? When we're not sure where we're headed, what can lead us is the hope that God has instilled passions in us – ones that He wants us to live into. He can lead us to the right opportunity.

The journey is part of the discovery!

Mallory Larsen

LOVE BEFORE FIRST SIGHT

Even before He made the world,
God loved us and chose us in Christ
to be holy and without fault in His eyes.

EPHESIANS 1:4

Have you ever seen (or experienced for yourself) parents preparing for the birth of their baby? Clothes, accessories and furniture are purchased, the nursery is set up, books are read and classes are taken. Parents attend countless doctor's appointments, attend parties in the baby's honor and excite over the flutters and kicks happening in the mother's womb. Almost immediately upon discovering that a baby is on the way, the lives of the parents are completely consumed with him or her.

Isn't that amazing? They haven't even met their child, yet they dedicate their time, money and energy to creating a safe and loving space for her, even before they've laid eyes on her. They may not yet know her name or her face, but they are attached in love to this new life. So it is with each of us; God anticipated our arrival, created a space for us and adored us before our face was even formed!

SPEECHLESS PRAYER

The Holy Spirit prays for us with
groanings that cannot be expressed in words.

ROMANS 8:26

Sometimes, our sighs are so big, so deep, filled with so much [insert your various emotions here], that our lips vibrate, our head falls back or our body collapses onto the nearest couch.

There is a lot happening in our worlds – more happening than we can always adequately express in words. When life feels full of anxiety, fear, depression, to-do lists, frustration or anticipation (the list goes on and on), we can soon be met with the limitations of language. Oftentimes, there are just no words.

God knows the boundaries of language and can identify the feelings wrapped up in our sighs, shouts and tears. Those, too, are prayer. We need not search for the most eloquent or appropriate words.

Speak to God from the depth of your soul, and bless whatever sighs or sentences come out. He hears them.

GO BIG!

The one who plants generously
will get a generous crop.

2 CORINTHIANS 9:6

Gardening is a significant time commitment. Planting seeds and then simply sitting back to watch them grow is, unfortunately, not how it works. We must tend to the dirt, water the seeds, ensure that there is sufficient sunlight, and protect the plants from hungry animals or disease. As can be expected, the bigger the garden, the greater the time commitment – and the more you reap!

The generosity with which we plant seeds (be it vegetables, flowers, friendship, etc.), the greater our return will be. If we want a lot of homegrown kale, loving friendships or a college fund for our child, we need to invest appropriately and regularly. We get out what we put into our work.

It is risky and difficult to invest deeply in our work and relationships, but imagine the richness of the gain!

JUDGED JUDGES

"Do not judge others, and you will not be judged."

MATTHEW 7:1

When you're with a friend who continually gossips about and judges others, do you ever find yourself wondering if she is saying similar things about you, when you're not around? What a horrible feeling! What do others deduce about us from the words we speak? Maybe we try to save our harshest comments about people for the ears of our closest friends, whom we trust with our dark thoughts. But, even still, regardless of who is listening, what do the words we speak say about our character?

When we judge others, we are opening ourselves up to being judged ourselves, not only by those who see our critical nature, but also by our Heavenly Father, who despises our judgmental thoughts and assumptions about others.

Our words inform others of our integrity and God will bring our words and thoughts to our attention, when we meet Him.

June 20

BURDEN-LESS, GRACE-FULL

*Finally, I confessed all my sins to You
and stopped trying to hide my guilt. I said
to myself, "I will confess my rebellion to the
LORD." And You forgave me! All my guilt is gone.*

PSALM 32:5

Few things weigh us down emotionally as much as an unspoken confession. When we know that we need to admit a failure or wrongdoing, but are paused by fear, the intensity of the burden we feel only grows. As time passes, the build-up heightens – how will they react; will they be able to forgive me; will anything go back to "normal" after I confess?

What happens when we finally do speak our misstep aloud? *My friend, I stole from you. My love, I lied to you. My God, I denied You.*

And then, we remain. The floor does not collapse under us, our heart is still beating, the earth is still spinning, and we are released, not of all our troubles, but of that burden. In fact, we may find that the fearful build-up was much worse than the dreaded confession! Grace abounds – with others, yes, but always with God.

June 21

LOVE IS ...

*"There is no greater love than to
lay down one's life for one's friends."*

JOHN 15:13

We will do some pretty wild things in the name of love! What would you do for the people you love? Would you wear a ridiculous outfit, move to the other side of the world or embrace your partners' favorite genre of music? There are really no limits when it comes to communicating our love.

What about giving your life for the love of another? It may be easy to tell someone, "I would die for you," but should the need arise, would you meet it? God tells us that giving our life for someone else is the deepest expression of love. This could mean literally dying in order to protect or save another. Or, we might "die to" our personal goals or comfort.

To love another means that their safety, health and comfort is greater to us than our own. It is a love like Jesus showed us!

June 22

Mallory Larsen

ONE WILD RIDE

Young people, it's wonderful to be young!
Enjoy every minute of it. Do everything you
want to do; take it all in. But remember that you
must give an account to God for everything you do.

ECCLESIASTES 11:9

Life is a real adventure. It is good to embrace this one wild ride on earth as much as we can. Be bold! Take chances! Try new foods! Go places where you never imagined you would; attempt things you never thought that you could. God didn't create breathtaking landscape, various foods or incredibly unique individuals just for us to sit around and be bored throughout each of our rotations around the sun. The world is full of wonders that are meant to be discovered and enjoyed.

How will you live with integrity, passion and vigor? In what ways can we take advantage of the invitation we've been given in creation to taste, to see, and to adventure? Maybe you've been feeling the urge to take that trip, write that novel or sign up for that salsa class.

Go! Do! Enjoy!

PLAYING WITH ABANDON

*"Dear friends, don't be afraid of those
who want to kill your body; they cannot
do any more to you after that."*

LUKE 12:4

Have you ever watched or played a game of paintball? Participants are divided into teams, given their own "paint gun" and released to try and hit the opposing team with paint from their gun, while avoiding being hit themselves.

It is a game that can often grow pretty intense, with players running, rolling and diving their way to safety. What's fun about this game is that the players participate with such energy, heart and fierceness. There is no fear that they will *actually* be fatally hit, so there is freedom to risk a bit more in the game.

We, too, are given the same freedom in our day-to-day lives. We know that, because of our hope in God, we will never face a final death. Though our body will one day fail, our eternity is a life with God. We can live for Christ with energy, heart and fierceness, because we know that no hit will take our life.

June 24

YOU COULD BE A MODEL!

You should imitate me, just as I imitate Christ.

1 CORINTHIANS 11:1

Who are the models in your life? Not the ones who walk the runway wearing today's latest fashions, but the ones who model something more eternal; the ones who show us what the fruits of the Spirit look like, when lived out well.

The ultimate model we have is Jesus Christ, whose steps we should all be seeking to follow. But we need modern-day models, as well, who will represent godliness and encourage us to continually pursue it. If you have a mentor like this, tell them how you see them and seek regular meetings with them. If you're without a godly mentor, consider looking for one in your Christian community.

The more we pursue Christ's likeness, the more we grow in His image and become a godly model for others!

COSTLY LADDERS

"What do you benefit if you gain the whole world but lose your own soul?"

MARK 8:36

Have you ever heard that life can be pretty lonely at the "top?" Why is that? Isn't "the top" where so many of us want to be at our job and in our social standing? The thing about the top is that, typically, there isn't room for a whole lot of people up there.

When we're focused on working our way up the narrow steps of the corporate or social ladder, we have limited space to even consider other things or people.

What are we making space for in our lives? If or when we do make it to the "top," what will we have to show for it? Will we be standing with good friends, rich experiences of fellowship and servanthood, and a close relationship with God? Or will we be alone, save for our money and notoriety? Do our pursuits match our values?

June 26

GIVING UNTIL IT HURTS

Honor the LORD … with the best part of everything
you produce. Then He will fill your barns with grain.

PROVERBS 3:9-10

We know that it pleases God greatly when we give to others. But how do we go about deciding what to give? When we come across someone who needs shoes, do we give them our favorite pair or the ones we like the least?

When someone is hungry, do we give them the last of our favorite food, or the cans in the back of the pantry that we'll never use? When we cross paths with someone who needs money, do we give them what we have left or wait until our next payday?

It is good to give, but all the more honorable when we give something we'll miss. Committing to giving to others means that, sometimes, it will hurt; but the impact that our generosity has on the kingdom of God is immeasurable. God promises to bless us for our generosity.

Practice faithful giving, trusting that even though sacrifices are made, we will be rewarded greatly!

CONTAGIOUS ATTITUDES

*Look after each other so that none of
you fails to receive the grace of God. Watch
out that no poisonous root of bitterness
grows up to trouble you, corrupting many.*

HEBREWS 12:155

Did you ever have chicken pox as a child? The highly contagious virus keeps kids (and some adults) nearly quarantined at home until the illness has passed. Being in the presence of someone with the virus who does so much as cough is enough to infect us with it. Clearly, it does not take much to catch it, but the treatment and healing process is a bit longer (and more painful!).

It is incredibly difficult to remain positive and hopeful in the midst of someone who is deeply negative and bitter. The weight of another's hope-lessness can begin to wear on us, slowly extinguishing our joy. Cynicism is quite easy to pick up, but can be much harder to move away from. If we remain rooted in joy, encouraging others to do the same, then our communities will be more inclined to spread contagious hope!

WORKING FOR PARADISE

Turn away from evil and do good.
Search for peace, and work to maintain it.

PSALM 34:14

Vacation time! We get to put away our work and responsibilities to spend a few days lounging at the beach or breathing in the mountain air. There are no to-do lists to work on, no meetings to attend and no emails to respond to. We are essentially free from all tasks and responsibilities in order to relax and rejuvenate.

Free from all responsibilities, that is, except for some. Regardless of where we are or what our day holds, no matter how hurried or relaxed our schedule is, being a light, a barrier of peace, and a vessel of love to others is a responsibility we should never free ourselves from.

Whether we are home or away, in the presence of friends or strangers, we should continually be striving to embody peacefulness and kindness. Vacation is a great time to rest, adventure and positively impact others!

June 29

SET APART

*You must worship no other gods, for the
LORD, whose very name is Jealous, is a God
who is jealous about His relationship with you.*

EXODUS 34:14

Our relationships, job and hobbies provide us with several different roles. We are friends, sisters, mothers, teachers, athletes, or artists. We are many of those, or just a few. To those in this relationship with us, we cannot be duplicated. We are someone's daughter, sister or wife; we are not one of many wives to our husband, or a faceless sister in a sea of siblings. We are unique, loved and valued.

There may be countless daughters, teachers or athletes in the world, but to those who know us, we are set apart.

God is not one in a sea of gods, but He is set apart, valued and certainly not capable of duplication. Though the relationship others hold with God may look different, the one we have with Him is particular to us. We should not look at Him as being just another god, for He certainly does not see us as just another woman.

June 30

July

WITH GRACE AND UNDERSTANDING

Jesus said, "Father, forgive them, for they don't know what they are doing."

LUKE 23:34

Being in the presence of a child who does not understand what is socially appropriate to say can be terrifying! Children are often known for being brutally honest – a trait that they consider harmless, while their caretakers are left explaining away the child's candid remarks. Who, though, can really blame a child when they say our dress is ugly or our hair looks bad? They have been taught to tell the truth!

We may be hurt, offended or shut down by those who do not follow Christ. It is painful or maddening, but can we really blame someone for acting outside of God's commandments when they don't know His teachings? Their behavior does not become less painful just because we come to an understanding of what they do not know; but let us treat these situations with grace and kindness, remaining hopeful that those who do not know Christ will someday see, hear and know!

ERASING THE DIVIDING LINES

"Any kingdom divided by civil war is doomed.
A town or family splintered by feuding will fall apart."

MATTHEW 12:25

It isn't exactly fun to be in the same space as someone we are fighting with. The temptation is often to (sometimes literally) draw a line, dividing the home, workspace or church in half. You can stay on your half, I'll stay on mine!

It might seem easier to avoid having to work out our differences with the person we're in conflict with, but there are other repercussions to our division. For one, we are no longer joining forces to share the load of our labor. We begin dividing tasks – keeping our distance from the chores, committees or departments that are not within our responsibilities and, soon, we're functioning separately, lacking the community, energy and potential of an entire team, family or church community.

When we can work through our differences, we grow in understanding and unity, doing life with others as God designed!

July 2

SOME THINGS NEVER CHANGE

He is the faithful God who keeps His
covenant for a thousand generations.

DEUTERONOMY 7:9

We all belong to a family of people who have gone before us in this life. We might be closely connected to our familial predecessors, or have little knowledge or understanding of who our relatives are. Some of us may be proud of the legacies we belong to; others may want to separate from them. Regardless of how fond or disinterested we are in those who walked this earth before us, isn't it amazing to know that God's promises were the same for them as they are for us?

Unlike values or norms, which may change over generations, God's vows to humankind will not shift, regardless of the context. We can count on His promises to be unchanging, no matter how much our world changes. Consider the people who were on this land hundreds of years ago; they, too, were cared for by the same God we know! What a sweet legacy to share!

July 3

WHEN FAILURE AND MERCY MEET

This High Priest of ours understands our weaknesses, for He faced all of the same testings we do, yet He did not sin. So let us come boldly to the throne of our gracious God. There we will receive His mercy, and we will find grace to help us when we need it most.

HEBREWS 4:15-16

We can all agree that it is no fun to fail. Disappointment, shame and doubt can easily flood us when we've set out to do something but are unable to achieve it. Is there a failure that you hold on to days, months or years later, that you're allowing to define you? Can you still feel now what you felt then – the pit in your stomach, the tears in your eyes or the disappointment, regret and rage in your heart?

Our failures are not the most important thing about us. When we lose a job, a race or a friend, there is pain and loss, but days, months and years still continue to come (and go!). When we allow our failures to define us, rather than shape and inform us, then we are not fully trusting in God's forgiveness or healing power. We will fail; and we will be met with God's mercy.

July 4

LEARNING TO WAIT

*Wait patiently for the LORD. Be brave
and courageous. Yes, wait patiently for the LORD.*

PSALM 27:14

When a friend is 15 minutes late to pick us up or our food at a restaurant takes a particularly long time to arrive, we can get a little antsy! We live in a culture of instant gratification. Emails and text messages can be received without delay, and easy access to the Internet allows news to spread across the globe in a matter of minutes. It's no wonder, then, that we are not particularly skillful at waiting – we so rarely have to do it!

Our fast-paced culture is not going anywhere, at least not for a while. We need to learn how to hold on to our patience while we live in a world where we so rarely need to use it. It will not be easy! Some good things come quickly, but many others come to those who can wait for them.

Waiting builds good character and trust in God – and anticipation!

July 5

TO REST IN PEACE

*How wonderful and pleasant it is
when brothers live together in harmony!*

PSALM 133:1

Have you ever cared for a group of siblings who simply could not get along? The constant screaming, hitting and taunting seems to be on an endless playback loop. Inevitably, the children soon cannot even remember why they started fighting or what they're really upset about, but they're too far in to quit now!

Silence becomes the sweetest sound when they are finally separated or put to bed, though you've already lost productivity (and some sanity), simply from hearing the conflict.

We can cause a lot of exhaustion, headaches and loss of productivity when we're in conflict with another. We may not be literally screaming and hitting one another, but when there is discord, it can impact many. Peacefulness is a much more restful and constructive way to live!

July 6

SWEET MEMORIES

"The seed that fell among the thorns represents those who hear God's word, but all too quickly the message is crowded out by the worries of this life."

MATTHEW 13:22

The first "I love you" in a new relationship, the excitement of a new job, or a powerful experience of God's presence. These are memories to hold onto! Soon, however, as the days pass and life continues to bring us worries and responsibilities, we can easily forget these sweet moments. Although that doesn't make these happenings less authentic, they become buried underneath more pressing concerns.

What a serious drag! We should be able to remember fondly the exciting moments that have impacted us, without the cares of our days fading our memories. Keeping reminders around that can bring those memories to life can be helpful. Keep a sticky note on your desk of the date your husband first confessed his love to you or revisit a journal entry you wrote after a time you experienced God's bold presence. Keep the truth of good memories alive, even in the midst of other work and worries!

July 7

REVIVED

Anyone who belongs to Christ has become a new person. The old life is gone; a new life has begun!

2 Corinthians 5:17

Have you ever seen news stories about a person being revived from death? For minutes, their heart is not beating. By all legal and scientific understandings, they are dead. But because of some determined medical staff (and heartfelt prayers), death does not win. The patient is brought back, their heart beating regularly, and their new lease on life has begun. Can you imagine leaving a hospital as a living being after being legally dead? What altered perspectives would you have; what different values would you hold?

In many ways, this is what it's like when we commit ourselves to Christ. We were once sinners with death as our ending, but now we are Christ-followers, saved by grace with eternal life promised to us! What different perspectives does this bring to your world? What values do you hold knowing that God has saved you from death? How will you embrace this new lease on life?

July 8

PLEEEEEASE!

"Keep on asking, and you will receive what you ask for. Keep on seeking, and you will find. Keep on knocking, and the door will be opened to you."

MATTHEW 7:7

"Mom, can I have a sucker? Mom, what about now? Pleeeeease, Mooooom?" A child can be relentless in their requests. They seem to think that the more they ask, the greater chance they have of receiving what they want. Exasperation is a favored tactic when it comes to kids asking for what they want.

While this may drive us up a wall to listen to, God appreciates this kind of persistence. We can be child-like in asking Him for things, continually naming our desires, no matter how repetitive we sound or annoying we feel!

As humans, our capacity for listening to incessant requests may be limited, but God delights in us telling Him the desires of our hearts. When we make the effort to ask God for things, we're showing Him that we not only believe He hears us, but that He can fulfill our desires!

A WORKING VACUUM

So you see, faith by itself isn't enough. Unless it produces good deeds, it is dead and useless.

JAMES 2:17

It is pretty clear when the vacuum cleaner is no longer working. All it takes is a swift push along the carpet to notice that it isn't picking up anything. If that were the case, would you continue vacuuming the house? Of course not! You would pause to fix the vacuum cleaner or get a new one, if need be. Either way, you would not keep vacuuming when the vacuum is not doing its job. What's the point?

Saying we believe in God but not living in a way that honors Him and serves others is rather futile. It's like taking the time to vacuum the entire house, but not actually cleaning it.

The words we speak mean very little when they are not supported by our actions.

Let's claim our faith in God and live as Christ-followers, lest our words be fruitless and our actions absent.

YOUR SEAT IS SAVED

"Don't let your hearts be troubled. Trust in God, and trust also in Me. There is more than enough room in My Father's home. If this were not so, would I have told you that I am going to prepare a place for you? When everything is ready, I will come and get you, so that you will always be with Me where I am. And you know the way to where I am going."

JOHN 14:1-4

Have you ever attended a "first come, first served" event? A concert, perhaps, that does not offer tickets, but only a limited number of seats. In order to see the show, you have to arrive at the venue several hours before the concert begins; and even then, you're not guaranteed a seat. What a stressful experience!

In the kingdom of God, there are no tickets, but there is unlimited seating. We don't need to worry about beating the lines or pushing others out of the way in order to get our place in heaven. We can rest in knowing that we are guaranteed a place at the table, and there is room to invite others as well! The urgency and anxiety in not knowing if there will be room for us can be silenced, because we are promised a place in the most heavenly venue.

GLIDING INTO GRACE

The LORD helps the fallen and lifts those bent beneath their loads.

PSALM 145:14

Not many of us are naturals at ice skating. Have you ever been on skates, courageously trying your hand at gracefully gliding across the ice? Did you fall, try to stand back up but then fall again as you attempted to get yourself vertical? It begins to feel like maybe we should just stay down on the ice because standing up again proves to be a nearly impossible task!

Sometimes it feels like life continues knocking us down until there is little motivation to get back up. We begin to think that if we just stay "down," we won't continue to get hurt; but that also means that we're not really living our life. We will face trials, but when we share our troubles with God, our fall will not only be softened, but it will be incredibly easier to stand back up again, with His help.

He will comfort and champion us to courageously overcome our falls!

July 12

FEARLESS LIVING

This is My command – be strong and courageous!
Do not be afraid or discouraged. For the LORD
your God is with you wherever you go.

JOSHUA 1:9

What would you do if you feared nothing? Imagine what sort of life would you live if fear simply was not a factor. Would you pursue a degree, spend a year volunteering in another country or start up the company you've dreamed about? Would you share the Gospel more often or love others more boldly? What would this life look like if we all lived as if there were life after death? (After all, isn't that the truth?)

God wants us to be responsible and wise, but He also wants us to be able to live without fear. If we trust in His presence and saving grace in our lives, then we can live fearlessly!

Inviting God to be in our life cancels out any reason for fear. What would you do if you feared nothing? Do it!

July 13

MELTING THE SNOWBALLS

"Don't worry about tomorrow, for tomorrow will bring its own worries. Today's trouble is enough for today."

MATTHEW 6:34

What does this day hold for you? Is it one full of meetings, projects and phone calls? Does the house need to be cleaned, do errands need to be run and how *is that bill due already?* What about the bill that is coming later this week? And the undertaking coming up at work next week? And, oh my goodness, the holidays will be here before we know it – there is much to prepare!

Our lists of to-dos, and the anxiety that comes along with them, can easily begin to snowball and, before we know it, we're worrying about hypothetical stressors that are not even a reality yet!

We are invited to take life one day at a time; God recognizes that we have enough on our plate for this 24-hour cycle, so let's focus on the things that this day holds. Tomorrow will hold new things – we'll be there soon enough!

July 14

CAUSE AND EFFECT

God's law was given so that all people could see how sinful they were. But as people sinned more and more, God's wonderful grace became more abundant.

ROMANS 5:20

We know that when there is a "cause," there will be an "effect." For example, we work out and eat healthy, so we end up losing weight. We study endlessly for an exam, so we get an excellent grade. Or we break the speed limit and then get a speeding ticket. Most cause and effect scenarios make sense (or we want them to, at least), with a positive outcome following a positive happening, and a negative outcome from something done wrongly or poorly.

There is nothing logical about God's grace. It is offered to us as the "effect" to our sin. Actually, it is the one "cause and effect" that we can count on, without question. There does not come a time when we run out of our grace-filled effects. While our sin may, too, have negative causations, such as legal or social reprimands, there will always be grace. Where there is sin, there is grace.

BREAKING CYCLES

"You have heard the law that says, 'Love your neighbor and hate your enemy.' But I say, love your enemies! Pray for those who persecute you! In that way, you will be acting as true children of your Father in heaven."

MATTHEW 5:43-45

What is your natural inclination when you are around someone who brings you pain or insult? Maybe you want to respond with an offensive comeback, tell another about how rude the offender is, or just run and hide from her. It's easy for us to react defensively when we're being treated poorly! However, there is another option for how we reply to those who try to bring us down. It may not be the most conventional or instinctive response, but it just might be the most memorable response for both the offender and the offended – and it is certainly the most godly.

What if, instead of responding to cruelty with cruelty, we, with boldness and courage, break the cycle of cruelty by responding to our offenders with love? What if we prayed for them, asked how they are doing or simply said we wanted to be in peace with them? Imagine the possibilities when hostility and love collide.

July 16

COMING SOON: JUSTICE

The LORD gives righteousness and
justice to all who are treated unfairly.

PSALM 103:6

It's difficult to "let it go" when something just isn't fair. Injustices of varying degrees can hook us; when we know that oppression and inequality are taking place, either personally or globally, we want to do something with the energy, grief and rage that boils within us. Are we supposed to just sit back when we know a child who is being abused by his parents, or when we read of the violent oppression of women happening across the globe?

We can (and should) take an activist role in addressing injustices, but we will not see absolute justice on this side of heaven. However, God promises that, one day, those who face injustice will be crowned with righteousness.

We cannot make right all of the wrongs of our world, but we can do our part to spread peace, part of which can be found in the promise that the oppressed will one day be blessed.

July 17

ACTIVE ENGAGEMENT

If My people who are called by My name will humble themselves and pray and seek My face and turn from their wicked ways, I will hear from heaven.

2 CHRONICLES 7:14

Consider the relationship you have with a close loved one – maybe a husband, sister or good friend. You spend time together, share your feelings with one another, and experience a level of trust and affection in the relationship. You feel safe sharing your desires with each other ("I'd love that bottle of perfume for my birthday"), admit when you've messed up ("I didn't listen when you shared about your day and I should have"), and continue to actively work on the health of the relationship ("I acted wrongly and this is what I'll do different next time …").

Our relationship with God is similar. It is not a stagnant relationship – we are to be actively engaging Him, speaking our desires to Him and admitting when we've wronged Him. It is a relationship we are to be constantly cultivating as we actively choose to turn towards Him with humility, trust and hope.

July 18

ALL ABOUT ME

*You are boasting about your own
pretentious plans, and all such boasting is evil.*

JAMES 4:16

Look at my new car! Guess what happened to me at work today! I am so busy these days! That fantastic new bag is all mine!

Have you ever paid attention to how many things you say that are all about you? It can be pretty easy to talk about ourselves; after all, we're with us every day! But, when sharing information about us shifts into boasting about our possessions and accomplishments, then we may become increasingly irritating to talk with.

The more we talk about us, the less we're inquiring about others. This way of being does not align with God's desire for us to love others well. How are we communicating our care or concern for others when nearly every sentence we speak contains "my," "me," "I," or "mine?!"

Share your life with others, but don't forget to make space for "you," "your" and "ours," not just "me."

July 19

HOPE IN THE WAITING ROOM

Let all that I am wait quietly before
God, for my hope is in Him.

PSALM 62:5

The waiting room of a doctor's office can be pretty bleak. Oftentimes, they are thick with anxiety, impatience, and illness; yet they are generally very quiet. In the silence of a waiting room, our fears, irritation, and desires for both freedom and healing are heard (even without being spoken).

We flip through magazines and play around on our cell phone, willing a nurse to come out and call us by name – to offer us care, hope and healing.

What sort of "waiting room" are you in right now? Maybe you're holding out for test results, a stable income or a partner to share life with. Whatever the wait is for, it cannot be easy. We try to pass the time, all the while hoping that God will appear, call us by name and lead us into healing.

Let the silence of your wait be filled with peace – our hope is heard; our name will be called!

July 20

COMMITTING TO JOY

*I can continue to help all of you grow
and experience the joy of your faith.*

PHILIPPIANS 1:25

Do you remember when you first learned to swim? Getting into the water without knowing how to stay afloat can be a pretty scary experience! However, swimming is an important ability to have, and so we are encouraged to "stick with it!" and continue to hone this skill. Eventually, our commitment pays off and swimming becomes somewhat natural to us. In fact, it even becomes fun! We swim away the days of summer, spending hours splashing, jumping and gliding through the water.

The more we begin to understand or grow oriented to something, the more space we have to enjoy it; our fear, anxiety or overwhelming distrust no longer obstructs our sense of peace, rest and joy. As we remain committed to God, we grow increasingly comfortable and, subsequently, increasingly joyful! There may still be difficult waters but, even then, we feel more capable of overcoming them. As our commitment increases, so does our opportunity for joy!

July 21

ONE MIND, MANY BODIES

*All of you should be of one mind. Sympathize with
each other. Love each other as brothers and sisters.
Be tenderhearted, and keep a humble attitude.*

1 PETER 3:8

It is a rather exasperating event to try and complete any sort of project with a person or group who have opposing visions for the work. How do we manage when each person on our team holds different priorities or values for the presentation being given or the party being planned? Tension escalates, confusion mounts and productivity suffers.

As followers of Christ, there should be little question about what each of our priorities or values are. If we, in our churches and communities, are focused on loving God and loving others, then the collective "how" of our work will reveal itself in time; meanwhile, even while in the process of planning or creating, we will be loving one another!

It's a blessing to be working with those who share our values, and it is what God intended for our collaboration!

July 22

THE MOST EFFECTIVE STAIN REMOVER

Create in me a clean heart, O God.
Renew a loyal spirit within me.

PSALM 51:10

Grease stains are the nemesis of nearly anyone who has spent some time in a kitchen! These stains are renowned for their staying power – most of us have little luck when attempting to remove even the smallest grease stain! What's important to note, however, is that, generally, they are possible to remove. It takes a great deal of patience, willpower, and the correct stain remover, but grease stains can come out of the clothing they soak into!

When we consider our poor decisions and missteps, it's easy to be discouraged by our "badness." We can start to feel too far gone, as if our heart, soul, and future are all covered in grease stains. While the wrongdoings from our past may impact us for a while, the shame and guilt we feel do not have to remain within us. No sin is beyond God's forgiveness; He can take care of it, no matter how "soaked in" it is!

FAMILIAR FACES

But Jesus spoke to them at once. "Don't be afraid," He said. "Take courage. I am here!"

MATTHEW 14:27

Who are your "people;" the ones whose support is invaluable to you? It may be your husband's partnership in raising your children, your best friend standing at your bedside as you're wheeled into surgery, or your family's presence at your solo vocal performance. If these faces are the ones that bring us strength and comfort, then what happens when they are absent? Do we lose our confidence when those who help instill confidence in us are not around?

When we find our confidence and strength in God, our sense of peace or level of performance is not dependent on His presence, because He is always with us. We absolutely need other people, but if, for some reason, our husband is working, our best friend is double-booked or our family is running late – even still, God is there. His strength, comfort, confidence and hope remains within us!

July 24

PLAYING BY THE RULES

We can be sure that we know Him if we obey His commandments.

1 JOHN 2:3

What rules must be followed in order to belong to certain organizations or institutions? We may need to pay dues to the gym, attend mandatory classes at school, or abide by a dress code at work. In order to live freely in our communities, we must abide by its rules, lest we spend our days locked up in prison.

Whatever the policy, we generally have an understanding that in order to belong to a particular community, we must meet its expectations.

Belonging to Christ is an invitation that is available to everyone! However, God has shared commandments with us that we are to follow as we commit our lives to Him.

There is no shortage of His grace, should (or when) we mess up, but just as we know we belong to a certain company when we wear their uniform, we can feel confirmed in our place in God's kingdom as we honor His commandments.

COMFORTABLE LOVE

Christ will make His home in your hearts as you trust in Him. Your roots will grow down into God's love and keep you strong.

EPHESIANS 3:17

Can you remember the early days of a now long-term relationship? What was it like as you were getting to know each other, growing in trust, comfort and affection? Eventually, as you spent more time together, a foundation of trust and respect is built, and you begin to integrate one another into your lives. His friends become your friends, your joy becomes his joy, and your two lives become shared.

The more time we spend with God – the more we invest in our relationship with Him – the more comfortable we begin to feel in the relationship. We grow in trust, comfort and affection and, eventually, there is a foundation of trust in the relationship. We start to believe that this God of ours really can save us. He really can bring us peace, strength, comfort and hope.

It is a relationship that takes time to cultivate, as all relationships do, but oh, how worthwhile it is.

July 26

DETAILS THAT MATTER

But the Lord said to her, "My dear Martha,
you are worried and upset over all these details!"

LUKE 10:41

Where does your attention go when you're planning an event? Do you worry about the food, the decorations, and the venue? Do you spend hours planning out the exact timing of the program, going over details that the attendees may never even notice or miss? How much time do we think about the practical questions of "who, what, when, where, how," without considering the impact of all of those questions?

Maybe, instead, we should focus on how people will see Jesus in whatever event we are putting on, be it a reception for 500 or a dinner party for 5. How will others know they are loved through the event you are hosting?

When we are thinking through the details of a dinner, party, or meeting that we are coordinating, let's consider the importance of the questions we are asking. What matters most in our work?

July 27

YOU LOOK LIKE ...

Jesus began teaching in the synagogue, and many who heard Him were astonished. They asked, "Where did He get all His wisdom and the power to perform such miracles? He's just the carpenter, the son of Mary and brother of James, Joseph, Judas, and Simon. And His sisters lie right here among us."

MARK 6:2-3

Imagine how jarring it would be to speak to a class-mate before the first class, only to find, when class begins, that your classmate is actually your *professor*. What was it that made you believe that your professor was just a classmate? What sort of assumptions were being drawn upon – did the professor look young; was she dressed too casually; was she hanging out in the "students' seating?"

It's so easy to allow our assumptions to inform our beliefs. If we are expecting our professor to "look like" a professor, then we're disallowing our relatively narrow assumptions to be broadened. We need to let ourselves be surprised by others. The person who looks like a student may be our professor, the one who appears to be our co-worker may be our boss, and the man who looks only like a carpenter may be the Son of God.

July 28

UNPACK-AND-GO

We brought nothing with us when we came into the world,
*   and we can't take anything with us when we leave it.*
So if we have enough food and clothing, let us be content.

1 TIMOTHY 6:7-8

Traveling by plane is not necessarily a restful experience. Navigating the airport and getting through security lines can be complicated enough, especially while lugging around our tightly packed luggage! It is a kindness to ourselves to pack light on our journeys. We may want to be prepared by toting along every item imaginable, but we're really hampering our experience by bringing so much stuff.

In life (and in the airport), we can get so weighed down by all of the stuff we acquire and insist on keeping with us, wherever our journeys take us. How much slower are we moving or how much more uncomfortable do we feel because of the collection of our belongings that weighs down our load? We will, at some point, get to a place where our luggage is not allowed, but let's consider what we can unpack and leave behind now in order to make our journey a bit easier (and more enjoyable!).

TO-GO BAGS TO SHARE!

God will generously provide all you need.
Then you will always have everything you
need and plenty left over to share with others.

2 CORINTHIANS 9:8

What do you do with the leftovers you have from a meal out? Do you leave them at the restaurant or take them home with you and forget about them in your fridge? Maybe you eat them for lunch the next day or give them to your dining partner to take home. Whatever your tendency is with leftovers, it may inform how we approach abundance in our lives.

When we have what we need to nourish us, the rest is abundance! It is wise to be resourceful with our abundance, such as saving leftovers for a meal the next day.

How, though, can we use our abundance to offer others a first course? If our one meal could be stretched into several (or we have plenty of winter clothing, school supplies or income), then let's consider how we can turn our abundance over to meet the basic needs of others.

July 30

DAILY DEDICATIONS

Commit everything you do to the LORD.
Trust Him, and He will help you. He will make
your innocence radiate like the dawn, and the
justice of your cause will shine like the noonday sun.

PSALM 37:5-6

It's always so sweet to read the dedication page of a book. Here, the author acknowledges someone (or several people) who influenced, inspired and/or supported the writer in her work. She dedicates the finished product as a way to thank and honor them for their impact.

What would it look like to dedicate our accomplishments to the One who influences, inspires and supports us to no end? God instills unique talents and inspiration within us, and to acknowledge this as we set out for or complete various endeavors is one way that we can partner with God and recognize His impact in our accomplishments. What are you doing today that you can dedicate to God? Let's invite Him to be a part of our work and thank Him for the abilities He gives us to do such things!

August

WORDS LIVED OUT

*What good is it, dear brothers and sisters,
if you say you have faith but don't show it by
your actions? Can that kind of faith save anyone?*

JAMES 2:14

Lifeguards are trained in rescuing drowning people and performing various lifesaving techniques, such as CPR. We all feel a little bit more at ease when we're spending a day at the lake with a lifeguard! But what if she says she's a lifeguard, but doesn't react when someone in the water needs help? She could have the sharpest lifeguarding skills imaginable, but if she is not willing to actually step out and be a lifeguard, using her skills and wisdom, then she will not save anyone.

Calling ourselves Christian is a bold statement. It implies so much about our values and desires. What sort of relationship with God and others should we have in order to live into the claims we make about our lives? If we say we are God-fearing Christians, but then doubt His love for us or question His ability to save us from our troubles, then do our actions really match our words?

August 1

A (WO)MAN'S BEST FRIEND

Love never gives up, never loses faith, is always hopeful, and endures through every circumstance.

1 CORINTHIANS 13:7

They are always excited to see us, rarely hold a grudge and remain steadfast in pursuing their desires. They keep asking us for food, even if they know it's a near impossibility, and they continue to return to us, even after we send them to the groomer. They comfort us when we're sad, play with us when we're joyful and serve as our constant companion, no matter the circumstances. We can learn a lot about love through observing our own dogs.

Loving others may not always be easy, but it is not necessarily complicated. When we're struggling with how to love someone, let's consider what our most loving and loyal dog would do.

We need to remain hopeful, even if our hopes sound completely illogical; we stay with our loved one, even when the going gets tough, and we believe the best about them (because we know it's in them).

August 2

PROMOTING PEACE

Do all that you can to live in peace with everyone.

ROMANS 12:18

What does it mean to live peacefully with others? What responsibilities do we personally hold in bolstering peaceful living? It may mean we smile at strangers or buy coffee for the person in line behind us; but it also means standing with those who are facing injustices in our world. Living in peace with others means that we not only practice peace, but we actively pursue it in and for our communities.

To bring peace to our world, we need to be a voice, speaking out about the places where peace is not and working with others to change that! We bring God, His love and His Word into our communities, not only through smiling at strangers and buying coffee for others (although those are great things), but we also need to advocate for people who are being treated wrongly and unfairly.

Our peaceful presence makes a difference, but we should help pursue it for others, too!

STAYING AFLOAT

*We are pressed on every side by
troubles, but we are not crushed. We
are perplexed, but not driven to despair.*

2 CORINTHIANS 4:8

When it rains, it pours, and when it pours, it floods, and when it floods, we begin to think that there is no place to go to escape the rising waters. Sometimes, life can feel like a line of dominoes collapsing, one thing directly after another. Where do we find hope when we're overwhelmed, feeling as if we're barely keeping our head above water?

We can persevere through difficult circumstances because of the hope that we may find a raft to float on, or a sturdy piece of wood where we can rest our head. Although total despair is always an option, particularly when all of the dominoes have fallen and we're left with nearly no stability, it does not have to be our only alternative. Hope can come in many tangible, albeit tiny, ways when we're feeling defeated.

Look for the small rafts, the warm sunshine and the hints of dry land ahead.

August 4

DARK SPACES, GOD PLACES

*Surely Your goodness and unfailing
love will pursue me all the days of my life.*

PSALM 23:6

Read a local newspaper, watch the world news, or walk down the streets of your own city. Pain and darkness are no stranger to this world. Actually, they reside in more places than we'd probably like to admit, and they can so easily cloud the joy of the Lord. Where is God in the poverty, violence and injustice happening oceans away from us and in our own home state?

It is oftentimes hard to believe, but God is there. He's in the villages with no food and little water; He is in the communities where women are being oppressed and children are being sold as slaves; He's in the schools being rampaged by shooters. He is with us, in the joy and in the suffering – He feels them both, too. He aches along with us (and celebrates with us).

Though pain remains very real, there is no place we go where God will not be.

THE RIDE OF A LIFETIME

He must become greater and greater,
and I must become less and less.

JOHN 3:30

Let's imagine that our lifelong dream has been to steer a hot air balloon high in the sky. Everyone would watch us bravely taking off, maneuvering the balloon with strength and sturdiness. Not only do we want to be in charge of steering the balloon for recreational purposes, but we also (secretly or not) want to inflate ourselves to a place of prominence, where we are seen and highly regarded by others for our work.

Let's say that, instead, God is chosen to steer. What a letdown for us!

But, oh my goodness, what if God has control of the gigantic balloon because He wants to use it to carry us where He wants us to go! We get to be along for the ride, but we remain human-sized, and God remains as big, powerful and holy as He is, controlling the way while empowering and supporting us in doing wildly amazing things!

August 6

SHARED THOUGHTS

The Lord is close to all who call on
Him, yes, to all who call on Him in truth.

PSALM 145:18

Have you ever called a friend who answered the phone by saying, "I was JUST thinking about you!" How cool is that!? There is an increased connection with someone anytime we learn that we were thinking about one another at the same time. These often feel like less of a coincidence and more like a God-inspired moment of closeness.

This is how it is with God, though instead of calling Him on the phone, we call to Him in prayer. Either way, His initial response to us would consistently be just the same, no matter how or why we're contacting Him: "Hi!" He'd say, "I was JUST thinking about you!" Regardless of how long it has been since we've called to God, He will have already been thinking about us, remaining close to us in mind and in spirit.

How does it change things to know that He's thinking about us – right NOW?

August 7

PROTECTIVE REFLEXES

Understand this, my dear brothers and sisters: You must all be quick to listen, slow to speak, and slow to get angry.

JAMES 1:19

Has the doctor ever checked your reflexes, knocking below your knee to see how quickly your leg kicks up? It's important for our safety to have quick reflexes; if we touch a hot stove, our reflexes will remove our hand from the burner before our brain can completely process what is happening.

What sort of reflexes do we have when it comes to anger? When someone hits a tender spot in our heart, stirring anger within us, do we immediately respond with harsh words or physical violence? Our reflex in anger should be such that our immediate involuntary reaction is something like a pause, a time to collect our thoughts and gather our composure. We should react with a willingness to listen to the other and calmly share our feelings. If our reflex keeps the situation from escalating, we may save ourselves (and the other person) from the hurt and regret of uncontrolled anger.

August 8

TOO ADAPTABLE?

You are following a different way that pretends to be the Good News but is not the Good News at all. You are being fooled by those who deliberately twist the truth concerning Christ.

GALATIANS 1:6-7

We humans are capable of adapting to various environments. If, for example, we moved from the east coast to the west coast, we will have to adjust to different weather patterns, accents and popular foods. It may seem uncomfortable for a while but, soon, we'll find that we are accustomed to the weather, acquiring the accent and cooking the local food dishes. What was once foreign to us has now become home.

What happens, though, when we become a bit too adaptable? We might begin altering our values and behaviors based on the group of people we are with. This is a slippery slope that can soon lead to hypocrisy and a loss of our sense of self. Who are we, without social adaptations for the sake of acceptance? Can we push back on what we disagree with and hold on to our sense of self and morality, regardless of whom we are with?

HUMILITY, HELP, HONOR

Humble yourselves before the
Lord, and He will lift you up in honor.

JAMES 4:10

What does it feel like when a child approaches you, eyes wide, asking for your help? Maybe he admits to not being able to do something on his own, or he simply wants to be picked up and comforted. It's hard to turn down such an honest, humble and innocent request – and why would we want to? It's an honor to be able to offer assistance, support and love to a child. After all, we are helping to shape their lives!

How, then, do you imagine God reacts when we approach Him for help? There is little difference between how we might respond to a child in need and how God would respond to us!

Humbling ourselves in order to receive help is actually incredibly honorable (partly because it is not always easy!); God will honor our humility and desire for His help, just as we should honor those who need our assistance!

ONE GOD, SAME PROMISES

This same God who takes care of me will
supply all your needs from His glorious riches,
which have been given to us in Christ Jesus.

PHILIPPIANS 4:19

When you see a neighbor down the street or a familiar but unknown face around town, do you ever think about how the water you get in your homes comes from the same source; your produce comes from similar farms; you are warmed by the same sun and sit under the same sky? It's fun to think about the things we share with people we have not met!

Consider, too, that the same God created you, your neighbor, the stranger in the grocery store and the men and women who walked the earth alongside Jesus Christ. It is the same God who knows you by name – and He knows the person who printed the pages of this book, the ones who bound it together and the ones who shipped it to the bookstore. Some things unify certain groups culturally, geographically or socially; God's love for and promises to us unify us globally, spanning all of time!

EXTRAORDINARY LOVE IN ORDINARY DAYS

That night the LORD appeared to Solomon in a dream, and God said, "What do you want? Ask, and I will give it to you."

1 KINGS 3:5

How sweet it is to receive unexpected reminders of loved ones. We may hear a friend's favorite song on the radio, then feeling prompted to call them, only later finding out that they had really needed to hear from a friend! Or you see a flock of seagulls – your late grandmother's favorite bird – and are flooded with happy memories of her. These can be such warm (and maybe not-so-random) reminders of dear people.

What sort of limitations do we have on how or where God can show up in our lives? Do we prepare ourselves to feel His presence most often in church, or hear His voice through Scripture? What if He's trying to nudge us through the flowers He puts in our path or the rainbows He paints in the sky? Maybe the crazy dream we just had was actually God-inspired; maybe He was trying to tell us something. Maybe most coincidences are not coincidental at all!

August 12

UNSPOKEN UNDERSTANDING

I want them to be encouraged and knit
together by strong ties of love. I want them to
have complete confidence that they understand
God's mysterious plan, which is Christ Himself.

COLOSSIANS 2:2

Have you ever made eye contact with another person and suddenly knew that you were both thinking the same thing, even without a word being spoken between you two? It's fun to be able to read someone like that and to share an unspoken connection based on your mutual understanding of a situation!

When we are with other believers, the unity we share in our faith in Christ is like the connection felt when having a conversation through eye contact! The Kingdom of God blesses us with a strong sense of togetherness because we have a shared belief in and understanding of Christ's sacrifice for us. While we, as believers, should be going out into the community, spending time with believers and non-believers, alike, we should embrace and value the unity that comes with faith in God!

August 13

VOICE RECOGNITION

*"The gatekeeper opens the gate for him,
and the sheep recognize his voice and come to him.
He calls his own sheep by name and leads them out."*

JOHN 10:3

You're walking through the grocery store, steadily making your way through the aisles while collecting items for dinner when you hear a familiar voice in the next aisle over. Without even having to see her face, you know, without a doubt, that it is a friend of yours. We can often make out a friend's voice before even seeing her face because we know her; her voice is distinct and familiar to us.

Are we familiar enough with God's voice that we could recognize Him as plainly as we do our friend in the grocery store? Is His voice distinct enough to us that we can identify when it is Him that is trying to get our attention or lead us somewhere?

The more we talk (and listen) to God, the more acquainted we are with His voice; when we know His voice, we'll know, undoubtedly, when it is Him who is leading us somewhere!

August 14

HAPPILY EVER AFTER

*"Here on earth you will have many trials and sorrows.
But take heart, because I have overcome the world."*

JOHN 16:33

Although we may already know the ending of a movie, it is still fun to watch! We can experience the suspense, tragedy and tension of the storyline, even though we are certain of the positive ending. Just because everything eventually works out does not mean that the beginning and middle of the story are not without action, surprises and heartache.

The same is true for our time on earth. We know the end of the story! We know that Christ will come back and that we will be saved from death – blessed by an eternity with God in His kingdom! However, that does not mean that we won't face tragedy, sorrows, difficulty and pain in our lives, even despite knowing the end of the story.

The best part about knowing the ending is that we can hold on to hope, even when the middle gets painful. The best is yet to come!

August 15

GENERATIVE GENEROSITY

"Give, and you will receive."

LUKE 6:38

You give a friend a present for her birthday; your friend gives you a present for yours! It's a social system that many of us follow – it might be the polite thing to do or it may be an unspoken cultural expectation.

Either way, when we give something, then we get something. Consciously or not, we may even be *more* inclined to give gifts to people that have previously given gifts to us.

God says that if we give to others, whether we have a relationship with them or not, then we will be blessed. We feel this when a friend gives a present to us after we gave one to them, but there is blessing for our generosity even beyond that.

When we give gifts, tithes and donations, our generosity will return to us, though it may not come from those we give to – God will meet our generosity with blessing!

August 16

NO FAVORITISM

*Remember that the heavenly Father to whom you
pray has no favorites. He will judge or reward you
according to what you do. So you must live in reverent
fear of Him during your time here as "temporary residents."*

1 PETER 1:17

Have you ever been friends with your boss? Outside of the office, you are peers, but at work, there are different boundaries – you are the employee, she is the boss. She cannot favor you over others, just because of your friendship. Because of that, there may be times when she has to discipline you or express disappointment in you based on your performance at work. This doesn't mean that she doesn't value your friendship, but that is simply the nature of the work relationship!

One day, God will judge us based on our behavior on earth. His judgment does not mean that He does not love us or value His relationship with us, but we cannot will ourselves past this aspect of the relationship, just because we love Him and He loves us. We need to remain mindful of our behavior on earth, for no level of closeness with God will make us exempt from His judgment.

August 17

A STANDARD OF GRACE

*Everyone has sinned; we all fall
short of God's glorious standard.*

ROMANS 3:23

What standards do you set for yourself? Maybe you expect to do things such as never missing a day of work, responding to every email within 24 hours, or reading every page of every book prior to every book club meeting. Whew! It's not very realistic to always meet the standards (however honorable) that we set for ourselves. In striving to live a life of integrity, we can set expectations for ourselves that leave little room for grace, resulting in us feeling like failures.

Before we were even born, it was written that all people have sinned. This is a truth that we are born into, so we can excuse ourselves from attempting to live a life of perfection, because that is a standard that we simply cannot meet!

We should strive to live a life of goodness – one that is sweetly pleasing to God – but we also need to recognize our limitations. Grace is here – breathe it in!

August 18

IMPENETRABLE LOVE

Give thanks to the LORD, for He is
good! His faithful love endures forever.

1 CHRONICLES 16:34

Love must endure a lot, particularly as imperfect humans seek to love imperfect humans. We hurt and disappoint one another more often than we'd like to admit. Have you noticed the limitations of your love? Is it when you are lied to, cheated on or abandoned? What atrocious level of disrespect and pain brings you to question your love for another? Is there something that would pull you out of feeling love for another person?

As imperfect people in relationship with a perfect God, we are guilty of hurting and disappointing Him. His love for us, however, endures the unthinkable. No level of abandonment, ridicule, anger or disrespect that we extend to God will interrupt His love for us.

When we feel weakness in our love, His remains strong for us. This does not give us permission to treat God recklessly, but if we do, His love for us will remain.

August 19

THE SOLID ROUTE

If you are wise and understand God's ways,
prove it by living an honorable life, doing good
works with the humility that comes from wisdom.

JAMES 3:13

Imagine that you have a choice between two roads to travel in order to get to your destination. One is filled with sharp turns, deep potholes and unexpected obstacles. It is dangerous, uncomfortable and scary. The other road, however, is smooth, well paved and relatively straightforward. There are no surprises and little danger; it is a route that is easier on our bodies and our vehicles.

Which would you prefer? Do you really even have to think about it?

If we live our lives committed to following God, we will be building a steady foundation (which we will continue to build upon). Our commitment to God will help to offer us a more stable road for the journey. That does not mean it will always be easy or without some bumps or wandering moments, but we will have the solidity of God's love, protection and promises to pave our way.

August 20

RHYTHMS OF GROWTH

The Holy Spirit produces this kind of fruit in our lives:
love, joy, peace, patience, kindness, goodness, faithfulness,
gentleness, and self-control. There is no law against these things!

GALATIANS 5:22-23

Gardening can be a fun pastime, though it is definitely a job that requires dedication! Different fruits and vegetables need varying levels of care at different times. At one point in the season, we may be focusing almost solely on our carrots, while another time in the season may call for more attention on our kale or tomatoes. That is a lot to keep track of, but what a relief that we don't have to try and focus intently on every item in our garden at the same time!

God cultivates fruits of the Spirit within us. They each take time, patience and discipline to grow. One season may call for more of a focus on growing our gentleness, while another season of life may require more devotion to cultivating our self-control.

Each of the fruits are in us, but will develop in their own time, with God's grace and our hard work and dedication!

August 21

SHADOWY FEARS

Even when I walk through the darkest valley,
I will not be afraid, for You are close beside me.
Your rod and Your staff protect and comfort me.

PSALM 23:4

What is scarier than walking in the dark, is walking in the dark alone. By ourselves, we feel more vulnerable and can more easily contrive noises and feelings into believing that we are in danger. Did you hear that? Is someone there? When we're with another, however, we feel the power in numbers – having someone with us helps to regulate our fears and imaginings.

When we are walking in the dark – either literally or figuratively – we can find strength and emotional regulation in remembering that we are never alone! God walks with us to both protect and comfort; so, how would our demeanor in the midst of darkness change if we remembered that no matter how dark it gets, we are not (now or ever) navigating the lightlessness alone? Do you believe the power of His presence protects you? May He ease our anxieties and surround us with peace, even (and especially) when night falls!

August 22

THE IMPORTANCE OF SHOWING UP

A friend is always loyal, and a brother is born to help in time of need.

PROVERBS 17:17

There are several ways to measure a good friend. Sometimes, however, being a good friend simply means answering the phone. Sometimes it is swooping in with little warning to take your friends' kids out for ice cream so she can get some sleep. It is saying, "yes," even when it is not your preferred answer. We may not be able to "fix" all of our friends' troubles, but we can be with them in the midst of it all – and that matters.

Being a good friend can often be boiled down to showing up. It is committing to being there for someone – to support and take care of them. That could mean calling them once a week, attending gatherings they host, championing them to pursue a big dream, or praying for them on a regular basis. Life is tough; we need each other. Let's not underestimate the power of showing up!

August 23

DOING THE UNTHINKABLE

Now all glory to God, who is able, through His mighty
power at work within us, to accomplish infinitely more
than we might ask or think. Glory to Him in the church and
in Christ Jesus through all generations forever and ever! Amen.

EPHESIANS 3:20-21

I can't believe I did that!

Have you ever accomplished something that you never thought you would have even tried in your lifetime? Did you go bungee jumping, travel alone to a different country, sing a solo at an open mic event, or write a book? It's so fun and satisfying when we are able to surprise ourselves with our own courage and abilities.

God also loves to surprise us, not only with the infinite number of things He can accomplish in our world, but also with the things He does through us. He instills within us the courage and ability to share His love with others in ways that might surprise us. Maybe you shared your personal story to a large group of people, moved across the world to serve God in a foreign country, or quit your job to do full-time ministry. What is He doing in and through you these days? Let yourself be awed!

August 24

THAT WHICH WE RECALL

*Don't be concerned about the outward beauty of
fancy hairstyles, expensive jewelry, or beautiful clothes.
You should clothe yourselves instead with the beauty
that comes from within, the unfading beauty of a
gentle and quiet spirit, which is so precious to God.*

1 PETER 3:3-4

Let's think back to a big event from our past – the senior prom, for example. Consider how much time and money was put towards having the perfect dress, shoes, accessories, hair and makeup. The entire ensemble had to be perfect for such a milestone event! Now, think back to your classmates who also attended the prom. Do you remember what they were wearing? Probably not. However, do you remember which girl from high school bullied you, or who came to sit with you when you were alone?

It is so easy to put a lot of time and money into our appearance, particularly for big events, but what we remember the most is how people made us feel; and we, too, will be remembered for that. Therefore, it is a far worthier investment to continue cultivating our character, rather than spending hours that turn into days concerned about how we look.

August 25

MERCY IS NO GAME

*Everyone who calls on the
name of the LORD will be saved.*

JOEL 2:32

"Mercy" is a game most often played on schoolyards around the world, where two children grab one another's hands and bend back each other's wrists until one person can no longer stand the pain and yells, "MERCY!" This is the cue for the other child to let go, therefore declaring them the champion. It's a horrible game, really, but the power and authority in the word "mercy" is noteworthy. This game of pain and surrender can sometimes be akin to the reality of life.

When things pile up and it feels as if our minds, bodies and hearts are being stretched and twisted in ways that feel far too painful and unmanageable, we can yell "MERCY!" to our holy God. We can call on His name, ask for His comfort, and experience His saving grace as it eases our pain and lifts our burdens. When life feels all but too much we can call out: "Mercy, Lord!"

August 26

NO MORE SHAME!

Let us go right into the presence of God with sincere hearts fully trusting Him. For our guilty consciences have been sprinkled with Christ's blood to make us clean, and our bodies have been washed with pure water.

HEBREWS 10:22

It is not easy to continue in relationship with someone after a conflict. When we have wronged another, the guilt and shame we feel can make it difficult to return to them, even after they have forgiven us. In moments when we do need to be forgiven, we should trust that when it is offered to us, it is a sincere offering. We can then return to our friend, coworker, or loved one knowing that our relationship can and will continue on, even after our mistake.

The same is true in our relationship with God. We can trust that His forgiveness is real. When we return to Him after sinning, we can return knowing that He does not just see our sin; He still wants to continue doing life with us, but without our shame! Whatever guilt we've been carrying with us can be set aside; we've been forgiven, and our relationship with Him carries on!

August 27

UNRETURNED TAUNTS

Never pay back evil with more evil. Do things in such a way that everyone can see you are honorable.

ROMANS 12:17

Have you ever witnessed the taunts of children spiral out of control? One child teases another; the other returns the teasing with further provocation. It does not take long before the two children are riled up, going after one another with passionate animosity.

One of the only things that will stop the hostile exchange is if an adult steps in and separates the two. However, wouldn't it be a catalyst to peace if, somehow, the taunted child chose *not* to return the taunts? How quickly the situation would be defused!

In what ways do we return the taunts of others in order to defend ourselves? It is hardly possible to imagine a world where no one would seek revenge to violence or mocking; but we can do our part to block the return of unkind words and actions.

Being a bearer of peace and godliness means we should not feed a heartless fire!

August 28

REFLECTIVE WORDS

*"The words you say will either
acquit you or condemn you."*

MATTHEW 12:37

Do you ever read the often hurtful or attacking comments on an online news article? Have you ever witnessed a debate on social media get out of control? Or have you sent a rage-filled email to a friend after a hard day? Our words can get ugly, particularly when we can let our computers or phones say them for us.

The words we use serve as a reflection of our character. Whether we're sending a text message, sharing our thoughts on social media or engaging in a conversation, what we have to say actually says a lot about the condition of our heart. Our words might seem fleeting, once we hit "send," but the nature of our language leaves a permanent imprint on our soul.

Before you share, ask yourself if your words are honoring to God, yourself and others. If they're not, hold off on sharing them and talk to God about what you're feeling.

August 29

SUPER-SIZED PEACE

You will keep in perfect peace all who trust in You, whose thoughts are fixed on You!

ISAIAH 26:3

There are no shortages of things to stress about these days. Circumstances regarding our finances, relationships and health are enough to keep anxiety around as our constant companion.

But it does not have to be this way! God desires to be closer to us than our own anxieties. The peace of God is greater than the stresses of the world, and that peace can cover us whenever we focus on Him. When we acknowledge that God is bigger than each of our worries, then we are inviting Him to bring us peace that will silence our anxiety. Sometimes, it just takes a deep breath and a whisper to realign our thoughts to God. Other days, we may be weeping on our knees, bringing our trust back to the Holy One.

Whatever your circumstances, God longs to step in and silence our anxiety with perfect peace.

August 30

ORIGINAL AND IRREPLACABLE

"I will never fail you. I will never abandon you."

HEBREWS 13:5

Think of all you rely on to work for you each day, often without giving it a second thought (until they don't work). The lights in your home, your car, and your body's senses are a few examples. While many of these often work for years at a time, everything worldly will one day perish (either permanently or until new batteries are installed).

If we so naturally rely on things that we know will one day fail us, what is stopping us from wholly relying on the One who is, who always was and who is still to come (see Revelation 1:8)? Many of today's technologies are incredible tools to aid in our everyday lives.

However, they are not replacements for God's presence. In fact, nothing is. So if the car won't start, the cell phone needs to be updated and the dishwasher is leaking, rest assured that God remains with you. Your deepest trust can be placed in Him!

September

HOPE WHILE IN THE DIRT

*When your faith remains strong
through many trials, it will bring you
much praise and glory and honor.*

1 PETER 1:7

It's easy to feel like "the grass is always greener on the other side," so to speak. Everyone else may appear to be living the life we desire while we feel deserted, unhappy or hopeless, living among dirt and pebbles rather than luscious green grass.

The truth is that comparing ourselves to others can cloud the reality of God's presence in our lives. Trusting that the journey we are on is our own, guided by God and crafted for us, can help turn the difficult points in our lives into blessings, knowing that they are shaping us. One of our friends may be experiencing a deep desire while we are grieving a significant loss. God has tailored each of our lives in such a way that we meet deep blessings at varying times.

God is with us, preparing our blessing for a later (and most suitable) time.

September 1

THOUGHTFUL SPEECH

A truly wise person uses few words; a
person with understanding is even-tempered.

PROVERBS 17:27

Are there people that you know whom, when they speak, everybody knows that they should probably pause to listen? It's likely that these people are prone to listen more than they speak, so when they do choose to share words with others, the rest of us want to listen because we know these words have been carefully chosen. When we take the time to process what it is we want to say, our words will be more thoughtful, true and honest. We will be speaking more from our heart and will be offering the wisdom and composure that comes with intently considering the words we speak.

This sort of thoughtfulness is particularly important when we are faced with emotional circumstances. Rather than speaking out of a knee-jerk reaction, our deliberate words will help to ground us in rationality. It would be incredibly difficult to say something regrettable if we consider so deeply the words we speak to others.

September 2

GRUMBLING TO GLORY

Our bodies are buried in brokenness,
but they will be raised in glory. They are buried
in weakness, but they will be raised in strength.

1 CORINTHIANS 15:43

Too short, too tall, too fat, too thin. Our face is too round, our feet are too wide, our fingers are too stumpy, our nose is too pointy. As if that doesn't give us enough we need to work through, our knees hurt, our back aches, our eyesight is poor and our balance is shaky. Allergies restrict our diet and chronic headaches impact our sleep. Whew!

Our bodies can give us a lot to grumble about. They take us on an incredible ride through this life, bringing us to see amazing places, valiantly working to fight off our infections and pain, and giving us the gift of our senses.

However, they cannot serve us forever. Eventually, our ailing bodies will cease to keep our lungs breathing or our heart beating. And, when that day comes, we can rest assured that our heavenly bodies will be a painless and perfect fit! Isn't that something to look forward to!

WISE INVESTMENTS

*Blessed are those who trust in the LORD and
have made the LORD their hope and confidence.*

JEREMIAH 17:7

We all want a reliable vehicle, but cars are expensive, so it's tempting to cut some corners and get something cheap! But then, shortly after our purchase, the brakes fail, the battery dies and the wipers only work occasionally. Now the car is not only unsafe to drive, but even more money will need to be put into it than we would have spent on a reliable, albeit more pricey, car!

There are many things or people that we can place our trust in. Committing our energy and trust into our best friend or handsome boyfriend may feel like the easiest decision, with a pretty sensible return for our investment, but how crushing is it when those humans, flawed like us, fail us?

Placing our trust in God may not always be easy – we have to trust and hope in an unseen being? How crazy is that? Crazy, maybe, but it is actually our safest and most fulfilling option!

THE POWER OF A NAME

*At the name of Jesus every knee should
bow, in heaven and on earth and under the
earth, and every tongue declare that Jesus
Christ is Lord, to the glory of God the Father.*

PHILIPPIANS 2:10-11

Encore, encore! At the end of a performance, this word, used by an extensive range of audience members, is shouted as a plea for the band or performer to play another song. With that word, performers know they are being summoned back on stage; it is a form of flattery and a passionate request, all within those six letters. "*Encore!*" is a call to action, understood by all involved.

One day, the name of Jesus will be a call to action that is honored by all. When it is spoken, we will be pulled into a posture of worship, awed by the peace that even the *sound* of His name can bring. It is one word, but one day, every person will hear this name and recognize the holiness, grace and life within those five letters. One day, we will all hear His reverent name as a call to pause, to worship and to love – and all will understand.

September 5

DEGREES OF MINDFULNESS

"Not a single sparrow can fall to the
ground without your Father knowing it. And
the very hairs on your head are all numbered.
So don't be afraid; you are more valuable
to God than a whole flock of sparrows."

MATTHEW 10:29-31

Many of us begin each morning by checking the weather report to prepare for how we will dress and what impact, if any, the conditions will have on our day. Will any of us notice, however, when the temperature rises by one degree, or if it is two degrees cooler than the weatherman reported?

God is an expert when it comes to attending to details. He checks on us like we check on the weather, wanting to know our disposition and how we will need Him each day. But He can also notice, with exactness, each tiny degree change. Our well-being is of the utmost importance to Him, but He can also notice, with precision, each tiny degree change. He has the capacity to be mindful of one single degree, or the impact of one gush of wind. He is a God of the big picture and the minute details – but we matter to Him the most!

September 6

COUNT ON HOPE

I waited patiently for the LORD to help me, and
He turned to me and heard my cry. He lifted me out
of the pit of despair, out of the mud and the mire.

PSALM 40:1-2

There are times when we all feel despondent; nothing is going right and hope is wearing thin. Maybe a loved one has passed away, we've been let go from our job, or our child is sick. In these places, hope feels far and the hole of anguish we are residing in feels deep.

We've learned in Scripture that we can call out to God and ask Him to rescue us when we are in a place of struggle. What is noteworthy is that we're told that God will lift us out of the pit of despair, which presumes that we will be there.

Hardships are not inescapable for any of us; however, when we find ourselves in difficult places (and we will), God will hear us and remind us how to hope, even when hope feels futile. Life will lead us into the pit of despair, but God will lead us out of it. This, we can count on.

THE VALUE OF HONOR

*Better to be poor and honest
than to be dishonest and a fool.*

PROVERBS 19:1

There are often stories on the news of wealthy businesspeople and politicians being arrested for laundering money. Many times, these people still have an income greater than we will ever see in our bank accounts, even before their dishonesty! Yet, that wasn't enough. When you have a lot of money, more can seem even more appealing.

We've all wondered what it would be like to have more money than we'd know what to do with, but if more money leads to the need for more, then the pursuit of money at all costs is hardly worth it. To live modestly but honorably will leave us with riches beyond this life, worth that far outweighs the money we could get our hands on now. Though lacking money is a worry for many, the weight we'd have to bear of living a dishonest and material-focused life is greater (and more dangerous) than most any other worry! Choose gratefulness!

September 8

Mallory Larsen

OUR OBEDIENCE, HIS DELIGHT

May our Lord Jesus Christ Himself and God
our Father, who loved us and by His grace gave us
eternal comfort and a wonderful hope, comfort you and
strengthen you in every good thing you do and say.

2 THESSALONIANS 2:16-17

It can be incredibly awkward when we say something to another that we consider to be thoughtful or meaningful, and they hardly respond at all. We might speak out about a word we heard from God or boldly offer encouragement to an acquaintance who we know is struggling. To take it one step further, we may even serve someone through a favor they did not ask for, such as bringing them groceries or sending a note and some bright flowers. These are profoundly kind offerings for others – and the kindness remains, even if our act goes unacknowledged by the recipient.

They may be speechless or simply overwhelmed; whatever the case, we look to God to fill us up for the acts of kindness we offer others. Let Him express His pleasure in our kindheartedness, and may His delight in us be more than enough to strengthen our spirit to continue serving others genuinely and selflessly!

September 9

HE STARTED IT!

We love each other because He loved us first.

1 JOHN 4:19

Isn't it incredible how there are some games and nursery rhymes that are known by nearly everyone spanning a nation, or several nations? Who began them and how do they spread? Slowly, a group of children catch on to a game, telling their siblings about it, who tell their friends, who tell their cousins, who tell their friends, and on and on. It takes a great deal of time and commitment (so it should be a pretty good game) to spread these things, but it happens!

God loved us before our body even existed on this earth; because we have His love, we are able to share love with our friends, our siblings, their friends, their cousins, and on and on.

His love can spread like wildfire, but only because He first showed it to us. He *is* love – love originated and exists within Him, but as He teaches it to us, we can offer it to others.

September 10

LIKE NEW

He has created us anew in Christ Jesus, so that we can do the good things He planned for us long ago.

EPHESIANS 2:10

Imagine buying a new dress and then, almost immediately upon getting it home, you accidentally rip the strap off of it. What a disappointment! Those are the moments we wish we could rewind to just a few minutes prior! Although the strap can be fixed, it will never be as good as new. Even still, after some sewing, we will still be able to wear the dress for years to come!

Just after the creation of human beings, sin took place and marred each of us. Though we are imperfect beings, we are not worthless, deserving of nothing but being cast aside. Jesus came and stitched us up; because of His sacrifice, we can be used for great and holy things.

Our sin does not make us ineffective; because of our new life in Christ, we can do great and impactful things in this world!

SHOCKING LESSONS

The Lord will guard you from the evil one.

2 THESSALONIANS 3:3

Invisible fences, buried underground, line the perimeter of a property and gently shock the family dog when he tries to cross it, training him to stay in his yard! Though the fence cannot be seen, the dog begins to learn where it is safe, and not safe, to wander, so the shocks eventually become fewer.

God is like our invisible fence, protecting us from temptation and attack from our enemies. Though we cannot see Him, if we remain mindful of His presence then we will be better able to discern when we are approaching dangerous territory, where deep temptation or a spiritual attack may reside.

As we learn what boundaries are safe for us, we can better honor those boundaries. They may frustrate us, but we need to trust that God knows (better than we do) what our limitations should be. He deeply desires to protect us, and He can be trusted to do just that!

September 12

YOU BELONG HERE

Stop telling lies. Let us tell our neighbors
the truth, for we are all parts of the same body.

EPHESIANS 4:25

It feels really good to feel like we belong in a group of people. It's nice to feel missed when we're not at an event, or for our presence to be appreciated. There is something deep within us all that so desires to be needed and wanted – a sense of belonging can often satisfy some of those desires within us.

Maybe you are not currently on a team, in a club, or an active part of a community. Even still, no matter where we are, however packed or empty our lives feel, we belong to a larger community. We are children of God, making up this wild and beautiful human race. We have a place here; our presence is needed here. Our neighbors and strangers matter to our lives.

We need one another because we can be God in the flesh to each other. If you feel like you don't belong, look around – we need you!

September 13

DEATH-DEFYING GLORY

*"Remain faithful even when facing death,
and I will give you the crown of life."*

REVELATION 2:10

Imagine, for a moment, a sickening scenario: a perpetrator aims a weapon at you and asks if you are a Christian. Your life is flashing before your eyes. This is it – your days on this earth will end here with an honest answer. Fib the truth, however, and you are given more time with friends and family.

What an honor it would be to be taken from this world while proclaiming our faith in God. If this were to be the case, our martyred body would be laid to rest, but our soul would be ushered into glory.

It is easy to say we are Christians while surrounded by Christians, but our faith in God should, without question, be bigger to us than our fear of man.

God has already defied death for us, so we can confess our commitment to Him boldly, even when facing death, because life is ours forever!

ROAD TRIPPIN'

Be strong and courageous! Do not be afraid and do not panic before them. For the LORD your God will personally go ahead of you. He will neither fail you nor abandon you.

DEUTERONOMY 31:6

It's hard to follow someone to a shared destination without having our own directions. What if only we get stopped at a red light, other cars get in-between us, or our friend simply drives too fast? We'd like to think that we will be following someone who will wait for us, should we lag behind, but there are many scenarios that could make it easy for something to go wrong, leaving us lost and alone.

What's hopeful about trusting in God's leading is that no amount of missteps or distractions will cause God to take off without us. He'll pull over if we get stopped at a red light (or if we decide we want to stop at some shops!); and He will slow down when other cars or distractions are particularly prevalent, so we don't lose sight of Him.

Following God may not always be easy, but we can trust that He'll stick around for the entire journey!

September 15

LITTLE OFFERINGS, BIG BLESSINGS

*Whatever you give is acceptable if you
give it eagerly. And give according to
what you have, not what you don't have.*

2 CORINTHIANS 8:12

I'll tithe next month, when I have a bit more saved up. I'll give to that organization next year, when I'm more established. I'll buy dinner for my struggling friend in a few weeks, once this month's bills are paid.

We can come up with many excuses as to why "now" is not a good time to give to others. However, the excuses will always be readily available. If we're in a tight spot financially, maybe we can just adjust how much we're giving, while still allowing ourselves to be generous with what we do have. We don't need to wait until we have a heap of savings to give (what if we never come up with a heap of savings?), but the spirit of giving can remain the same, regardless of how much we have to offer!

Even if our offering cannot buy much, the generosity we're showing to others is a priceless gift.

September 16

GOOD DEEDS, RIGHT HEART

People may be right in their own eyes,
but the LORD examines their heart.

PROVERBS 21:2

Growing up, did you do the exact chores (and not one extra) that were asked of you, when they were asked of you, with some complaining on the side? Do you begrudgingly attend your mother's Christmas cookie decorating party every year; or did you go to the conference that your boss asked you to attend, but complain about it via social media the entire time? What things do you do because they are the "right" things to do; and are we still doing the "right" thing when we are doing it resentfully?

We could go through a lifetime of doing good deeds and, at the end of our life, be standing before God and hear of His disappointment for those same deeds we considered "good."

How does that make sense? Well, because our heart matters! The condition of our heart and our attitude all contribute to making a good deed, good.

September 17

PASS IT ON

"Shouldn't you have mercy on your
fellow servant, just as I had mercy on you?"

MATTHEW 18:33

Are there any heirlooms in your family – a piece of jewelry or furniture, for example – that has remained in the family for countless generations? What an honor to have the piece one day passed down to you.

When the time comes, however, for you to hand it down to your child, would you consider simply not handing it over? Not only would that be selfish, but it would also be pretty senseless! The piece is not yours; it is the family's. It was given to you freely, with the understanding that you, too, would give it over freely. It's pretty hard to justify why you wouldn't!

God offers us mercy without us having to earn it, so how could we justify requiring others to earn our mercy? Since it is so freely given to us, can't we, then, so freely give it to others? Because we have so generously received it, we can so generously give it!

September 18

LOVE THAT STRETCHES

No power in the sky above or in the
earth below – indeed, nothing in all creation
will ever be able to separate us from the love
of God that is revealed in Christ Jesus our Lord.

ROMANS 8:39

Have you ever played with putty? It can be stretched, twisted, shrunken or enlarged, but it is not easily broken! Regardless of what tangled things we do to it, even if we break it into pieces, it will reattach, returning once again to its original state.

Our bond with God is similar, but all the more strong. Christ's sacrifice on the cross immediately solidified an unimaginable love. Our rejection, un-awareness, or death cannot even put a dent in rupturing God's love for us. Whatever knotty or convoluted things we try to do with His love, however much we will it to break into pieces, God's love can withstand any circumstance.

Even our physical attempts to separate ourselves from His love are futile; if we decide not to take it or shape it in our own lives, it's still not going anywhere. It can bend to reach nearly impossible circumstances, but it will never break!

September 19

HEART COMMITMENT

I press on to reach the end of the race
and receive the heavenly prize for which
God, through Christ Jesus, is calling us.

PHILIPPIANS 3:14

Running a long race is tough on our spiritual, mental and physical capacities. We need to be committed to the long haul; any significant waver in commitment will make it easy for us to quit. What keeps you "in it?" Is it the emotional satisfaction, the medal, or the food at the finish line?

Our faith journey is also no easy feat; it is filled with obstacles and difficult stretches. It requires our commitment – commitment that may waver somewhat, but enough of us – 51% of our heart – must continually believe that the journey to an eternal life with Christ is worth the effort. This journey is not always the easiest way to get through life. We will not glide through it unscathed. We must overcome doubt, fear and anger. There will be heartache, intensity and honorable lessons. But we take this journey, because at least 51% of our heart knows that it is the most worthwhile way to go.

September 20

INCOMPARABLE SIN

The person who keeps all of the laws except one is as guilty as a person who has broken all of God's laws.

JAMES 2:10

Have you ever read the police report in the newspaper? Someone was arrested for speeding, drunk driving, driving on a suspended license and driving without insurance – all of that in one traffic stop! Goodness, that is quite a list of offenses! Then, we think to ourselves how proud we are of only having ever received one, single speeding ticket. What a glowing record! And, in the eyes of the law, it's true – we'd be considered a safer driver.

God, however, does not compare our varying levels of sin. One "little" sin and several "big" sins are still just that: sins! When we begin comparing our sins, as if there are "okay" sins and "bad" sins, then we're sinning further by being so prideful.

We should be striving to live a life that pleases God, while still knowing that we will fall short. We're all on the same playing field – we're sinners who are saved by incredible grace!

September 21

HELP WITH HEALING

*Confess your sins to each other and pray
for each other so that you may be healed.*

JAMES 5:16

If we slip and fall down the stairs, breaking our leg, what do we do? That's not much of a question, is it? We do whatever we need to do to get ourselves to a doctor who can help relieve our pain and set us on a path towards healing.

It would be painful and challenging to heal from something like that on our own, with no medical intervention or support from others. It might be possible, with great precision and tolerance for pain, but why not receive help?

When we let others in to the areas where we have fallen short, we can, with their help, support, and wisdom, be aided in relieving the pain, recuperating from the shame, and moving away from our sin.

Bringing those we trust into our process can offer us deeper care and encouragement as we learn from our missteps and move forward!

September 22

PEACE IS HERE

*"I am leaving you with a gift – peace of mind
and heart. And the peace I give is a gift the world
cannot give. So don't be troubled or afraid."*

JOHN 14:27

Spas and tropical vacation packages advertise peaceful escapes from reality. Because our lives are so chaotic and peace often feels so absent in our world, businesses have begun advertising peace-filled experiences to others; it is a pretty hot commodity!

While a day at the spa or a weekend at a secluded B&B would be incredible, deep peace is actually found in trusting God with our troubles and believing that He is taking care of us. One of the perks of His peace is that we don't have to vacation for a weekend to get it; it can be found while we're in the midst of the chaos: our kids are screaming, we're late for a meeting and our babysitter just canceled. Nothing about that sounds peaceful, but God's peace is different than what the world offers – it is peace that depends not on our surrounding environment, but on allowing Him to reside in our hearts.

September 23

LOVING WHO HE LOVES

If someone says, "I love God," but hates
a fellow believer, that person is a liar; for if
we don't love people we can see, how can
we love God, whom we cannot see?

1 JOHN 4:20

Imagine getting to work for a woman you deeply admire. She hired you at her company because she trusts that you will be a dedicated employee who cares about the values and mission of her organization. Maybe you are not yet completely immersed in the mission of the company, but you serve wholeheartedly because you have so much respect for your boss. Through your commitment to her, your passion for the work will grow exponentially!

Our love for God should be evident in the way we interact with others, because those others are so deeply loved by Him, too. We want to please Him and be delighted in by Him, just as we would want to please and honor our boss. Out of our genuine love for God comes our genuine love for His people, not because we feel like we have to love them, but we want to, as we are so taken by His love for us!

September 24

LIGHTING THE WAY

*Do everything without complaining and arguing,
so that no one can criticize you. Live clean, innocent
lives as children of God, shining like bright lights
in a world full of crooked and perverse people.*

PHILIPPIANS 2:14-15

Have you ever traveled down a house-lined street at night that didn't have street lamps? It gets surprisingly dark on those roads. Our car's headlights light a bit of the path ahead of us, but we are still left with incredibly low visibility. This becomes increasingly frightening when the street is a winding road or is lined with children playing outside beneath the stars. Street lamps are always helpful in guiding our way and keeping everyone safe.

What does it mean to be a "light" here on earth? Being kind to others, offering help and guidance, committing to help keep others safe, and desiring to lead and be lead in living an honorable life – these are some characteristics that light us up in this dark world.

When we live like this, we will be like street lamps on an otherwise dark road, doing our part to light up the way.

September 25

GROW AS YOU GO

*Learn to do good. Seek justice. Help
the oppressed. Defend the cause of
orphans. Fight for the rights of widows.*

ISAIAH 1:17

If we want to live a life rich with good deeds, then we need to allow our lives to be about other people. Upright lives are not necessarily lived by first changing or cultivating our character – that will happen in the process of serving others. If we seek justice, help those in need and defend the defenseless, then we will, at the same time, be shaping our character to be more like Christ's.

When participating in a marathon, which takes months of training before running the race, we train first and then run the race. In our Christ-centered life, however, running the race is our training! We will learn, serve, and grow as we are in our faith journey.

Our heart for serving God and others does not mean that we first wait until we've got our lives together; serve now, and watch the fruits of the Spirit within you grow as you go!

September 26

FREEING UP OUR MIND

*"Don't worry about these things, saying, 'What will we eat?
What will we drink? What will we wear?' These things dominate
the thoughts of unbelievers, but your heavenly Father already
knows all your needs. Seek the Kingdom of God above all else,
and live righteously, and He will give you everything you need."*

MATTHEW 6:31-33

What does your pantry look like? Is it filled to the brim with cans and dry pasta? Are you one to stockpile your food, to ensure that you will never run out? Take a look at your closet; are you stockpiling your jeans or shoes, too?

The more we think about the availability of things like our food and clothing, the more obsessive we can become and, soon, we are controlled by what we're wearing or how prepared we are with canned goods, should we be stuck at home in a storm.

God knew our needs as children, and they were fulfilled back then. He continues to know our needs now, and will meet them, even without our worrying! Imagine what we can do with the extra space in our minds when we trust God to be our provider. What *else* could use your mind's focus? Let it go there!

September 27

I BELIEVE

*"I tell you the truth, you can say to this mountain,
'May you be lifted up and thrown into the sea,'
and it will happen. But you must really believe
it will happen and have no doubt in your heart."*

MARK 11:23

Do you believe in miracles? We read of them taking place in Scripture, and even hear of them happening, but do you believe you could actually witness a real, God-inspired miracle? If you meet a paralyzed man who so desperately wants to regain his ability to walk, do you believe that, if you pray in the name of Jesus, that man could walk again?

Our faith in God should be big enough to include our belief that He can work some serious miracles. That doesn't mean that He will perform all of the miracles we request (but He could). The paralyzed man may not stand up and walk after our prayer; does that mean he never will? Maybe he'll be healed in hours, years, or only once he reaches heaven. That is not for us to decide, but as we continue to pray for miracles, let's watch what happens as we're actively living out our faith!

September 28

LEADERS WHO LOVE

*"Among you it will be different. Whoever wants
to be a leader among you must be your servant."*

MATTHEW 20:26

Watch any politician on the campaign trail and you will probably see them doing things like dishing out food at a soup kitchen, building a neighborhood playground or serving smoothies to patients in the cancer ward. This is not to say that those politicians are not doing these acts out of the goodness of their own hearts, but why are they done so publicly?

Well, we, as voters, like to see that the person who is leading us is also just like us. We want to know that although they have authority, they can come down to our level, serve us and care for us. We don't want to be under a leader who uses his power for self-serving motives.

We want leaders who use their power to love others! This is the kind of leader Jesus was, disallowing His divine power to be used for ill but, instead, using His influence to impact others with His love.

September 29

WHAT ARE YOU THINKING?

Those who are dominated by the sinful nature think about sinful things, but those who are controlled by the Holy Spirit think about things that please the Spirit. So letting your sinful nature control your mind leads to death. But letting the Spirit control your mind leads to life and peace.

ROMANS 8:5-6

Can you imagine what it would be like if we could see each other's thoughts, as if the content of our mind was broadcast on a live feed above our head? That would be bizarre and uncomfortable, but does the mere thought of it take you directly to feeling terror or shame? What kind of person would others see you as if they could see your thoughts?

The things that fill our mind are the things we're investing in (if a relationship, movie, or dream job is always on our mind, that says something). We need to do the work of being proactive in controlling our thoughts; doing so will keep us living upright, godly lives that are pleasing to Him and honoring to ourselves. When our thoughts are pure, we can enjoy them shamelessly and embrace the ability to think, dream and imagine! What are your thoughts saying about you and your values?

September 30

October

COPYCATS

Don't copy the behavior and customs
of this world, but let God transform you into
a new person by changing the way you think.
Then you will learn to know God's will for you,
which is good and pleasing and perfect.

ROMANS 12:2

Children are often quick to copy others – especially siblings. If we imitate our brother or sister who is misbehaving, we may be quick to jump on the defense: "Well, Mom, *she* did it first!" Mom, frustrated, then so thoughtfully responds, "Well, if she jumped off of a bridge, would you?" That tends to be a real conversation killer because, no, of course we wouldn't! So why, then, did we copy her misbehavior?

We have no shortage of people to follow in our lives. Take a look at the various decades of fashion trends throughout centuries past; many of us are, at least somewhat, following one another! While that may continue to happen with the ways we dress or do our hair, God is the one we should be copying in our thoughts and actions.

The more we seek to copy Him, the more we will grow to be like Him!

October 1

ACCEPTANCE OF THE UNSEEN

*We understand that the entire universe was
formed at God's command, that what we now
see did not come from anything that can be seen.*

HEBREWS 11:3

When looking at a house, we cannot know *all* of the materials and processes that went into building it. Without having witnessed the step-by-step process of building the house, from the creation of the materials, to their delivery and setup, can we still trust that the house is legitimate, man-made, and worthy of appreciation? We probably see the name of the builder and don't think twice about it!

We could not see the process of God forming the universe. We do not know what it looked like when the core of the earth was formed, or when the ground below us and the sky above us came into being. However, we trust that our world is legitimate, God-made and worthy of appreciation – we see the name of the builder in Scripture and need not think twice about it! We were not a part of the building process, but now this earth is ours to enjoy – what an incredible gift!

October 2

LOOSE LIPS

A gossip goes around telling secrets, but
those who are trustworthy can keep a confidence.

PROVERBS 11:13

It is such a disappointment when our favorite coffee mug begins to leak. Initially, we might pick it up from the table and see a ring of coffee where it had been sitting. That's too soon to give up on it, so we continue to use it; but we soon find that the leaking not only persists – it worsens. Eventually, we are forced to admit that this mug can no longer be used for coffee-drinking purposes.

Are you one to remain trustworthy and dependable when your friends share with you their thoughts, feelings and secrets? Or, do you slowly start to leak things, telling one person, and then another? After a while, your friend will learn that you are not trustworthy; she may continue to spend time with you on some level, but will hesitate to return to you for the purpose of sharing her feelings.

Let's be friends who place a seal around the words entrusted to us!

October 3

MERCIFUL DIRECTIONS

*We make this plea, not because we
deserve help, but because of Your mercy.*

DANIEL 9:18

We're several hours from home, hoping to make the drive back before it gets too late. Heading out, we realize that we're not sure where we're going, a tire is low and our cell phone battery is nearly dead. After stopping at a gas station, we notice that we need the help of a stranger for all of our troubles (*Will you give me directions? Can you help fill my tire? May I use a power outlet to charge my phone?*) What warrants us to ask for all of this when we clearly do not deserve so much selfless assistance?

Well, grace warrants it! We have to believe that we all care about one another's well-being enough to do what we can to serve another in need, friend or stranger. We know we have done nothing to earn God's mercy. He bestows it upon us freely because He loves us so deeply.

As we, too, love others, may our grace simply abound!

October 4

FALLING INTO GOD

The eternal God is your refuge, and
His everlasting arms are under you.

DEUTERONOMY 33:27

Have you ever done a "trust fall," falling backwards into the arms of another, yet not knowing when they were going to catch you? As the name suggests, the crux of the activity is trusting that the other person will, in fact, catch us. It can be a terrifying game (though relatively helpful, should we want to know which of our friends are physically trustworthy!).

When we meet difficult or overwhelming circumstances, we begin to feel like we're falling backwards, uncertain who is going to catch us (or when!). When we put our trust in God, however, we believe that He will catch us; and that His arms will remain under us, holding us up from falling any further into the pit of despair.

In those spaces, when it's hard to feel like anything is going right, our safety and well-being can be found in His presence. We may have fallen, but we were caught!

October 5

REDEMPTIVE BEAUTY

Continue to show deep love for each other,
for love covers a multitude of sins.

1 PETER 4:8

It is so redemptive when a neighborhood turns a downtrodden, previously dangerous piece of land into a beautiful garden where neighbors can enjoy the flowers and fellowship of others. Suddenly, a place that once held so much violence, fear, anger and darkness becomes a place that holds new life, beauty, and friendship.

Every time we choose love over hate, any moment when we decide to encourage rather than insult, it is as if we are turning darkness into new life. We are sinners and we will continue to fail, but our love for one another can speak louder than our sins. When we love, the light wins out – whatever darkness we've contributed to our world cannot hide from the light. We can bring redemptive love to our relationships and our communities every day.

How can you create redemptive beauty in your community today?

October 6

CHOOSING GOD'S HELP

This is what the LORD says: Do not be afraid!
Do not be discouraged by this mighty army,
for the battle is not yours, but God's.

2 CHRONICLES 20:15

Have you ever been told to "choose your battles?" If we were to act on or respond to every word or action that provoked us, even in the slightest, then we'd spend most of our entire lives acting on or responding to those words and actions that provoke us!

When in relationship with God, choosing our battles becomes all the more important – and much easier! There will certainly be circumstances that we will need to respond to in our lives, but God can guide us in how to do so. No "battle" needs to be chosen (or not chosen) without His help. He wants to relieve us from the attack and anxiety that comes with approaching our enemies alone. Next time we're faced with a battle, take a deep breath and choose to let God into the situation. The battle is no longer our own – God is in it with us, and He will lead us out of it!

October 7

BETTER THAN COOKIES

"If you sinful people know how to give good gifts to your children, how much more will your heavenly Father give the Holy Spirit to those who ask Him."

LUKE 11:13

Let's say, for a moment, that you are a renowned chef. One day, your child comes home from school and says, "Mom! My teacher knows how to make sugar cookies and she made some all by herself and brought them for us to eat. Do you know how to make sugar cookies?"

"Um. Well. Yes, honey," you may respond, while knowing that you not only have your own special sugar cookie recipe, but you are able to create much more than that in the kitchen!

God looks at us and says, "You! You are imperfect, yet still can offer good things to others. So imagine what I can offer, as a perfect God!" That's pretty hard to argue. We humans can usually do a generally acceptable job at caring for one another, but a God who does not fail would do a perfect job. That makes trusting Him pretty hard to pass up!

October 8

PERFORMANCE REVIEW

*A day of anger is coming, when God's
righteous judgment will be revealed. He will
judge everyone according to what they have done.*

ROMANS 2:5-6

There is often some anxiety when it's time to receive our final grades from school or quarterly performance review at work. Everything we have done for the past several months will be critiqued and analyzed, our intent for our work being taken into account slightly, but the actual impact of our performance will be weighed most heavily. We know we have not done a perfect job, but hope to have been "good enough" to receive encouraging, positive feedback.

At the end of our life, we will again face a sort of performance review from God, though it will go over the ins and outs of our time on earth. There will be things we did well and things we could work on, but isn't it helpful to know that this time with God is coming? We know now that our behavior on earth will meet a final judgment, so there shouldn't be too many surprises!

October 9

KNOWN, THEN SEEN

I knew you before I formed you in your
mother's womb. Before you were born I set you
apart and appointed you as my prophet to the nations.

JEREMIAH 1:5

A big event is coming up and you know the *exact* dress that will be particularly perfect for this party. Although you have not yet found the dress, you can picture it in your head; you know what it looks like and are certain that nothing will fit this occasion better than this dress. But, first, you need to either find it or make it!

On a deeper (and more meaningful) level, God could picture us before we were even born. He had big ideas about the things we could do and the places we could go that would fit us (and our abilities) just perfectly throughout our lives. He knew the skills we would have and the ways that He desired we would use those skills for His kingdom. Even before He laid eyes on us (and even before we had eyes), He knew us and had hopes of how we would add beauty to the world.

I'M [NOT] FINE

If you are bitterly jealous and there is
selfish ambition in your heart, don't
cover up the truth with boasting and lying.

JAMES 3:14

"I'm fine. I promise; nothing's wrong! I'm actually glad that you were given the job and not me. I'll get so many better opportunities; that job actually sounded really awful!"

Our jealousy and bitterness can lead us to deny the truth of our feelings. Nobody wants to come across as being jealous or bitter, but the alternative of being dishonest is far worse! Hiding our true feelings only blocks us from engaging those feelings; and it prevents others from joining us in what we're going through (and, the truth is, we're probably not fooling anyone with our untrue defenses). It may not be realistic to say that we will never feel jealousy, but what we can do is prepare ourselves for the moments when we do feel jealous.

How will we notice our jealousy and be honest about it, rather than trying to defend ourselves with bravado and untruths?

October 11

HITTING BUMPERS

Make allowance for each other's faults,
and forgive anyone who offends you.

COLOSSIANS 3:13

When we "toddler-proof" our homes, setting up bumpers on the corner of furniture and cabinets, we are essentially communicating to our child, "I believe that you can and will walk just fine, but I also know that you'll fall sometimes; and, when you do, I want you to be as protected as possible." We are making room for our child to slip and fall without it being something they cannot recover from.

Our relationships need bumpers, too. We need to let each other be human-sized – glorious, unique and imperfect. We will fault one another, but maybe, in our fault, we'll hit a bumper instead of it being an irrecoverable relational misstep. If we were to withhold bumpers of forgiveness from everyone who has wronged us, we may soon become pretty lonely people.

We need to let forgiveness have a place in our relationships – not only because others deserve a chance after they fail, but because we do, too!

PARTIAL COMMITMENTS

Love the LORD your God, walk in all His ways,
obey His commands, hold firmly to Him, and
serve Him with all your heart and all your soul.

JOSHUA 22:5

Imagine getting up in the air, however-many-thousand feet, to skydive, only to decide that you don't want to jump, politely asking to be taken down to land.

Later, you decide you do have the gusto to jump, so you get back on the plane but, again, you decide not to take the plunge. Over and over, you ride up in the plane but back out at the last second, afraid of the risk, danger and uncertainty of jumping.

It's hard to live our life for God when we're only partially committed to Him. We might think we're "all in," but when something risky, scary, or unknown happens in our faith journey, we may want to bail. If this is the case, we'll never really go anywhere. We'll never experience the fullness of the wildness and adventure of living life with God, nor will we find out what happens when we take the leap into full-on commitment to Him.

October 13

ALIGNING OUR PASSIONS

All who fear the LORD will hate evil.
Therefore, I hate pride and arrogance,
corruption and perverse speech.

PROVERBS 8:13

Do you start to feel more passionate about particular things as you grow in your relationship with your partner? Maybe you despise a particular sports team because he does; you swear off peanut butter because he is allergic; or you begin to dislike particular holidays or hobbies that bring him painful memories. When we love someone, we want to bring them delight – and we want the things that don't bring them joy to disappear! We know that life will hold pain, but we want to do all we can to ease or remove any amount of it!

Our love for God is no different. We desire for Him to be honored and, with that, we want to do our part in removing whatever behaviors hurt or displease Him. The things He despises, we despise – and we should actively do our part in ridding ourselves of such behavior. Let's grow passionate in that which He is passionate about!

October 14

OPENING THE FLOODGATES

May the Lord make your love for one
another and for all people grow and
overflow, just as our love for you overflows.

1 THESSALONIANS 3:12

It's no secret that there is too much hatred, hurt and violence in the world, but do we ever hear others complaining that there is too much *love*? In a world filled with cultural, political, racial and religious divides, it's hard to believe anyone would argue that we are surrounded by plenty of love. Actually, could we *ever* have an *abundance* of love, or will there just always be room for more?

The hope is that, one day, we will be in an environment that is submerged in love. That day, however, is not today. But we can do our part to bring little sprinkles (or big splashes) of love into our communities, with the hope that others will do the same.

Who knows – with a whole lot of sprinkling and splashing, love may begin to flow more vigorously around us until, one day (definitely in heaven, but maybe on earth!), we're totally submerged in God's sweet love.

October 15

BEING NOTICED

You yourself must be an example to them by doing good works of every kind.

TITUS 2:7

Take a look at today's idols in popular culture: movie stars, musicians, athletes and socialites. While we cannot judge the condition of their heart, the media portrays the values of many of these icons in such a way that pulls us away from God's values. In popular culture, the emphasis is on fame, money and sex appeal. None of these are very in line with God's ideals!

We may not have as wide of an impact as celebrities, but people are watching us. Those in our midst see the way we live our lives and wonder about whether or not it's worthwhile.

What is the purpose and the profit of committing our life to God? Although our influence may not reach as far and wide as that of our culture's idols, imagine the one or two (or several) lives that could be changed because our life reflected Christ's.

October 16

SHARING HOME BASE

Share your food with the hungry, and give shelter to
the homeless. Give clothes to those who need them,
and do not hide from relatives who need your help.

ISAIAH 58:7

Oftentimes, our home feels like "home base." We're done; we made it! Our work is over! We did what we needed to do for the day, and now we get to sit down, relax, and relish in our accomplishments of the day.

Our generosity, however, should not have a close of business hours. Can we open ourselves up to being continually prepared to serve others, even if that means leaving the comfort of our home base for an evening, or letting someone come over and stay in our house? It's quite neat and orderly when our generosity is planned out, but we need to make space for the unplanned moments; for the times when we're in our pajamas, the doorbell rings, and our friend is there, struggling and alone, needing support and a refuge. It is wonderful to have quiet and relaxing evenings, but when we are open to serving others in unexpected moments, anything can happen!

October 17

ALTERNATIVES TO RUNNING

When I am afraid, I will put my trust in You.

PSALM 56:3

When we're happy, we smile. When we're surprised, we jump. When we're attracted we move close. When we're grieved, we cry. When we're embarrassed, we blush. When we're afraid, we … what do we do? We might run, hide, scream, or fight as instant reactions upon feeling fear. But let's consider a different response. What if, when we're afraid, we trust in God?

It may feel easier or more beneficial to run when fear hits us, and we can do that, but if we are first putting our trust in God through whatever fearful situation is upon us, then we may not feel like we have to run quite as fast or as far (or maybe we won't even have to run at all).

Trusting God through the scary things can pull us up from the anxiety that leads us to want to run, hide, scream, or fight. Afraid? Trust God – and save yourself the run!

ASK, ANTICIPATE, CELEBRATE

*Each morning I bring my requests
to You and wait expectantly.*

PSALM 5:3

Do you remember how exciting it was to make a Christmas or birthday wish list as you were growing up? (Maybe you still make those lists – and it's still just as exciting!)

There is so much joy and anticipation in creating those lists! Why? Because it's exciting to think that we might actually get some or all of the things we're asking for. What if we get one thing on our list? What if we get *everything*!

Every day is an opportunity to make a wish list of our needs and desires. While the people around us may get weary of our lists, God will not; in fact, He wants us to bring our desires to Him!

Every moment with Him is an opportunity for us to speak our hopes and needs, and then wait and see what happens. What if we get something we're hoping for? What if we get it all? What sweet anticipation!

October 19

CONSIDERING OUR WEALTH

*You know the generous grace of
our Lord Jesus Christ. Though He was
rich, yet for your sakes He became poor,
so that by His poverty He could make you rich.*

2 Corinthians 8:9

What is it that you are rich in? Believe it or not, we're all rich in something. It may be money, but consider other things, as well, such as pride, anger, or self-contempt. Maybe you consider yourself rich in joy, laughter or courage! Our riches could even vary with our seasons of life.

Christ came and gave His life so that we may be rich in joy, hope, peace and love. These are the things He wanted for us to have in abundance when He came and sacrificed Himself for us.

What are we doing with these riches He has offered us? Are we ignoring them and instead remaining rich in bitterness or doubt; or, can we enjoy the riches given to us by God through Christ, recognizing that no matter how much money we have, being rich in the fruits of the Spirit is the utmost extravagance!

October 20

NEVER SAY NEVER!

You are a holy people, who belong to the Lord
your God. Of all the people on earth, the Lord
your God has chosen you to be His own special treasure.

DEUTERONOMY 7:6

What sweet memories do you have of times when you were chosen – chosen to play on a team, to be someone's date or to work a particular job? What about painful memories of experiences when you were not chosen (Those memories are often louder than the sweet ones.)? For many of us looking back on our lives, it's easy to think, "I never get chosen for anything!"

To that, we can say, not true, dear souls! We are chosen – and by the God of the universe, no less! It can be too easy to forget this truth as we're going through our days, but let's do ourselves the service of reminding not only ourselves, but others, too, that we are chosen to be God's children – to be vessels of His love to others.

While it is undeniably painful not to be chosen for a job or a team, we can remember that we have been chosen for life everlasting!

October 21

A LIVELY RELATIONSHIP

Be joyful. Grow to maturity. Encourage
each other. Live in harmony and peace.
Then the God of love and peace will be with you.

2 CORINTHIANS 13:11

Have you ever been in love? When we're in a deep relationship with someone, how does it change us or shape us? Loving relationships often make us want to be better people. We want to grow in maturity, wisdom, patience and affection with (and for) this person. Not only do they inspire us to grow, they help teach us (and they grow with us).

The same is true in our relationship with God. When we come to feeling complete awe at who He is, we are inspired to grow and mature in our character, faith and relationship with Him. We want to please Him and show Him that we're committed to the relationship.

Loving and being loved by God should transform us. It is not a stagnant relationship; it is one that moves us towards holiness, honor and gratitude. How will His love shape you and move you today?

October 22

NOT ALONE

Stay alert! Watch out for your great enemy, the devil.
He prowls around like a roaring lion, looking for someone
to devour. Stand firm against him, and be strong in your faith.
Remember that your family of believers all over the world
is going through the same kind of suffering you are.

1 PETER 5:8-9

Suffering is awful. Suffering alone is a pain beyond words. We face struggles in life that others may never experience. However, we do all have struggles; although we each have our own brand of struggle, we can empathize with what it's like to simply face trials. When we let God and others into our "brand," we are no longer fighting our struggle alone!

To be a child of God and to walk this earth means that we will face hardships. We will meet attacks from those who are against God and our work with Him for the Kingdom. Though we all may experience these attacks in different forms, remember that we are all experiencing them. We can share in that, and we can help one another to remain encouraged. God, too, is with each of us, so while our struggle can feel lonely, it does not have to be. Join and be joined - we are not alone.

October 23

GOOD HAPPENINGS

*We know that God causes everything to work
together for the good of those who love God and
are called according to His purpose for them.*

ROMANS 8:28

You miss your flight to a critically important work event, and will likely be heavily disciplined. Later that day, however, there is a fatal earthquake in the area of the event. Your job security may have been risked, but your life was saved.

Sometimes, when things don't go according to plan, we assume that they have gone "wrong," and we grieve the loss of what should have been. However, sometimes something does not go according to plan, but deep blessing ends up coming from the unplanned happenings!

Things will not always work out in the way we want them to, but things will work out for our good. God has already written the end of the story. We have been saved and His focus remains on our best interest. He, however, has better ideas than we do about what is best for us. We can trust Him with those details and anticipate the "good" to come!

October 24

SAFETY IN THE BANDAGE

*He heals the brokenhearted
and bandages their wounds.*

PSALM 147:3

If we get a deep cut on our arm, we need to keep it bandaged in order to stop the bleeding and protect it from further harm. That bandage is a dead give-away – when people see it, they know we've been injured and are in the healing process. However, it can also bring us some measure of peace. With it on, we feel more protected – there is a layer between the outside environment and the susceptible cut.

When our heart is aching, God wants to serve as a bandage for us. He wants to come alongside us and be the presence protecting our hurting and vulnerable heart from the harshness of the outside environment. He will tend us back to health, not promising that there will not be a scar, but helping us to believe that healing is possible, particularly with His assistance.

The healing process is not a quick one, but it is infinitely easier with merciful care.

October 25

UNBROKEN PROMISES

*Do not tremble; do not be afraid. Did I
not proclaim My purposes for you long ago?
You are My witnesses – is there any other
God? No! There is no other Rock – not one!*

ISAIAH 44:8

Are you surprised when someone follows through on a promise they made? "I can't believe you actually did that!" We say. And then, dumbfounded, they respond with, "Well, I told you I was going to!" It is a sad reality when we find ourselves surprised by kept promises. Yet, the truth is, we fail one another. There are times when we don't keep our word. Consistency in promise keeping can be rare among our relationships.

God, however, does not want us to be surprised by His kept promises. There is no need! When we're afraid or lost, He has told us to trust in Him because He will show up for us. We have to wonder if we're letting Him show up for us? Are we so doubtful that He'll keep His promises that we don't even wait around to see Him do it? He continues to keep the longest-lasting promises; watch Him hold to His word!

DO GOOD!

The life of the godly is full of light and joy,
but the light of the wicked will be snuffed out.

PROVERBS 13:9

It feels good to do good. When we have performed well at work, surprised a friend with a gift or served someone in need, we just feel good. When, however, we're doing things we know are wrong – we steal something from the grocery store, spout off a rude comment to someone, or betray our loved one, we are burdened.

Whether we are consciously aware of it or not, the shame mounts itself on us. We are not full of light and joy, even if that is how we act. We have pockets of darkness and shame in us that will not dissipate by simply ignoring them.

Living a godly life is not only pleasing to God and honoring to others, but it brings us fullness of life. We get to have the privilege of sharing love with one another; there is deep joy and goodness in that – more than we will find in our sins!

October 27

LITTLE FEATS, BIG THANKS

As soon as I pray, You answer me;
You encourage me by giving me strength.

PSALM 138:3

We often expect a lot of ourselves and can be easily disappointed if we don't meet our expectations. What, for example, is on your to-do list today? What are the things that must get done, and what are the things you'd like to get done?

In the midst of so much to do and so much not yet done, we need to be able to celebrate the "we did it!" moments.

When we're asking God for help to do the things we want to do, He may respond by helping us to do only the things we need to. Maybe God gave us the strength to get out of bed this morning and feed our family breakfast. Well, guess what – that's a win. On days when we're weary, even the simple things are no small feat.

Celebrate when you (and God) have accomplished what you need, and have grace for yourself when you have not accomplished all you wanted.

October 28

PLEASURE OR PAIN?

*Haughtiness goes before
destruction; humility precedes honor.*

PROVERBS 18:12

Have you ever seen an accident coming before it happens? You notice, for example, that a car is not slowing down as it approaches a line of stopped cars at a red light; or you see that your child's flailing arms are getting dangerously close to her full cereal bowl. You can't act quick enough to stop these events – all you can do is grimace and brace yourself for what's about to occur.

When we witness unabashed arrogance and selfishness, it's easy to think that someday, either tomorrow or years from now, that sort of behavior is going to bring pain or regret. When we live a life of humility and kindness towards others, we are stepping more fully into being the kind of people God created us to be – and that is deeply honorable.

If we're living an arrogant life, we need to brace ourselves for the destruction it will cause our relationships; kindness, however, will bring pleasure!

October 29

A LOVE-FILLED COOL DOWN

*Hatred stirs up quarrels, but
love makes up for all offenses.*

PROVERBS 10:12

Have you ever lost track of a boiling pot of water? You're in the kitchen with countless other distractions and, before you know it, you look over and the pot is boiling over, spilling hot water all over the stove. However, as soon as you lift the pot from the burner, everything simmers down and the water stops pouring everywhere. The pot simply needed to get away from the heat.

Conflicts can escalate incredibly quickly. Before we know it, we're engaged in a heated yelling match that is undoubtedly going nowhere. One act of love in a situation such as that, no matter how small the act, will be like removing the pot of boiling water from the heat. It will calm the situation, bringing a pause, along with some peace and stability to those involved.

Love, which can be expressed in countless variations, can calm even the most intensely passionate conflict.

October 30

ANXIOUS FEELINGS

Don't worry about anything; instead, pray about everything.
Tell God what you need, and thank Him for all He has done.

PHILIPPIANS 4:6

How are you active in your anxiety? Do you bite your nails, lose sleep or get stomach aches? We all feel and express our anxiety in particular ways. Some of these ways may be incredibly obvious, and some we might do or feel without even realizing it. How do you think anxiety manifests itself in your world?

What if we actively engaged our anxiety through prayer? Rather than letting it swirl around in our stomachs, or losing all of our fingernails to the stress, what if we allowed our anxious feelings to move us into a time spent with God, where we offer Him our feelings, ask for help and express worship and gratitude for who He is.

We need not stop where we are and get on our knees every time an anxious feeling arises; our prayers can be fluid throughout our day. As we drive to work, sit in a meeting or make dinner – prayer can happen there!

October 31

November

GOOD SURPRISES

"If you give even a cup of cold water to one of the least of My followers, you will surely be rewarded."

MATTHEW 10:42

When have you been surprised by the unexpected? A stranger pays for your coffee, an old friend you haven't heard from in years sends you an email to say hello, or someone you hurt a long time ago shows up to attend the memorial service of your loved one. These are all unexpected but incredibly loving and honorable actions.

Small things can carry great impact, especially when done by the people we'd least expect. Who are the people who would least expect a good surprise offering of love and kindness from you? Maybe it's someone from your past who has hurt you, or the man you pass on the street every day who is begging for change.

Our acts of love towards them do not need to be massive, but the little things can communicate great love, particularly when they're offered to the most unsuspecting child of God.

November 1

Mallory Larsen

INEXPLICABLE JOY

I know the LORD is always with me. I will not be shaken, for He is right beside me. No wonder my heart is glad, and I rejoice. My body rests in safety.

PSALM 16:8-9

It's wonderful to have days when we're in a particularly good mood for no apparent reason; no major event happened, it's not a holiday, a birthday, or a day filled with big and exciting plans. It's just ... a day, and we are grateful and excited to be living it!

It's a wonder why we allow days like that to be so few and far between. The truth is, we always have a reason to feel as if we're bursting with joy! God's presence and protection in our lives should give us a lot to smile, jump, yell and celebrate about!

There is (and generally always will be) much to grieve in our world, but we are all the more qualified to step into the grievous places of people's pain if we consistently take the time out to recognize how worthwhile (and necessary) it is to share the joy of the Lord with others!

November 2

CALCULATED FALLS

*Now all glory to God, who is able to keep you
from falling away and will bring you with great joy
into His glorious presence without a single fault.*

JUDE 1:24

Have you ever watched bungee jumpers (or been one yourself) leap off of tall bridges, falling hundreds of feet down before the bungee they are attached to stretches to its limit and they bounce back up, (*before* hitting the ground at a dangerously rapid pace)? It's a risky pastime, but the jumper trusts that they will be protected because the bungee cord is just short enough that they will not be able to fall too far to where they would hit the ground.

Sometimes, life with God can feel like we are attached to a bungee cord. There are moments of risk and fear, but we remain close enough to Him that we will not hit the ground at a fatal rate. He releases us to go and do the things that He has for us to do, but He never lets go of us.

November 3

AT FACE VALUE

Don't forget to show hospitality to strangers,
for some who have done this have
entertained angels without realizing it!

HEBREWS 13:2

How many times do you think you've walked past a celebrity on the street or in the airport? Maybe you've even been in the same room as your favorite singer or actor without even realizing it! What would have changed about your behavior or presence in that room, had you known that a celebrity was standing just feet away from you?

There is nothing regular about anybody in our world. We are all wonderfully unique beings and deserve to be noticed, approached and cared for. In opting out of smiling at a stranger or saying "hello," we could miss our chance to meet an unrecognizable celebrity and we'll certainly miss out on our chance to show kindness to a stranger! When we love everyone well, it will not be possible to have "missed opportunities," should we be in the same room as one of our idols, because we will be taking advantage of our opportunity to love all people!

November 4

A SWEET FAMILY

So it is with Christ's body. We are many parts
of one body, and we all belong to each other.

ROMANS 12:5

What's it like in your home when one person is in a horrible mood? It sort of ruins the cheerful vibe of the house, doesn't it? Everyone knows that something is wrong with that one member, and it's not desirable to continue on happily when one is hurting. We want to assist the one who is struggling, coming alongside them to offer support.

The kingdom of God is a great big family, and not all of us are going to always be okay. When that is the case, what do we do? Do we just ignore the hurting members and go on with our day, or do we pause to listen, support and encourage those who are struggling? We need one another (sometimes you'll need me, other times I'll need you).

This family should pick us up when we're having a hard time – it is, indeed, one of the sweetest parts about belonging to a love-filled family.

November 5

THE "WHY" OF OUR WANTS

*Even when you ask, you don't get it
because your motives are all wrong – you
want only what will give you pleasure.*

JAMES 4:3

Think about some of the things you've asked for throughout different occasions in various seasons of your life. Did you want a particular toy because of its enticing commercial, a certain pair of shoes because everyone was wearing them, or a new car – to make your friends jealous? Many of us rarely take the time to think about why we're asking for what we're asking for, but it's a helpful question!

When we bring our requests to God, do we ever pause to wonder why the request is ours in the first place? Do we simply want to fit in or make others jealous? No matter the request, we should consider what it is in our heart that desires to see this prayer be answered.

God already knows the condition of our heart, but if we're not seeing an answer to our prayer, we may know why, when we consider our motivations!

November 6

UNRESTRICTED TRUST

God is our refuge and strength,
always ready to help in times of trouble.
So we will not fear, even if earthquakes
come and the mountains crumble into the sea.

PSALM 46:1-2

Where do you draw the line when it comes to trusting God? Consider the scariest thing you can imagine. Maybe it's easy to trust Him with the "somewhat scary" stuff, but when we start getting into this "unthinkably scary" stuff, we back away a little bit and wonder if He's worthy of ALL of our trust. God happens to believe that He is worthy (of it all).

What if the ground you are standing on right now just fell out from underneath you? Falling, unsure of where you're headed, would you still be able to put your trust in Him? We shouldn't need to trust God conditionally. He is not a semi-powerful, semi-all knowing, semi-holy God. He is all of all of those things, and no matter how much terror we face, He is capable of showing up and catching us, even if the ground is literally taken out from underneath us.

November 7

JOY IN THE ACTION!

*"Ask, using My name, and you will
receive, and you will have abundant joy."*

JOHN 16:24

Do you ever have one of those mornings when nothing seems to be going right – the internet isn't working, your coffee spills everywhere and, worst of all, your child simply will not stop screaming. Joy feels nonexistent in those moments. Yet, what if we considered the blessing of having the internet in our home, access to hot coffee and a healthy (albeit loud) child? What good gifts, that can bring great joy!

Prayer can lead us to frustration, especially when our prayers feel unanswered. However, what if the act of prayer, alone, brought us joy? Consider what a blessing it is to have a God whom we can pray to! That should create joy within us! We can share our requests with God, acknowledging our desire to live by His will; then, we wait to hear and see what He does with our requests, knowing He has our best interest in mind.

What an invitation into joy!

A PART OF THE PARTY

"Where two or three gather together as My followers, I am there among them."

MATTHEW 18:20

What do you bring with you when you gather together with friends? Maybe you bring a dessert; you might have photos to share from the previous weekend, or stories of your life's latest happenings. You probably bring a bit of your stress, frustration or sense of accomplishment from the day. And, it's probable that all of your other friends are bringing similar things, too. That's a room full of food, stories, and feelings!

What we might soon forget, however, is that God is there, too. He is alive within us and comes with us wherever we go! Where we are gathered, particularly in a room full of believers who acknowledge and invite His presence in their lives, He is there to bless, encourage and be actively engaged in our relationships. What does it change to remember His presence in the room? How can we kindly receive Him into our fellowship with others? Acknowledge Him, welcome Him, thank Him!

November 9

MORE IS IN STORE!

You have turned my mourning into joyful dancing.

PSALM 30:11

After a difficult breakup or a job loss, we are in desperate need of some cheering up. Few things, however, sound as if they'll do the trick. We certainly don't want to celebrate our losses, but what if the pain of our loss could be coupled with the (joyful?!) anticipation of things to come!

If retrospect wasn't so "retro," we could sooner understand that the pain we're experiencing may actually be unto something good! It could be that better things are in store because of our movement away from that job or relationship. We need people who can remind us that more is in store for us – whatever painful occurrence we're experiencing is not the end of our story.

Our mourning is valid, but it should also be paired with some sense of anticipation for the new opportunities that we now have room for in our lives. God can lead us from grief to goodness in His divine timing!

November 10

(UN)CONVENTIONAL LOVE

"Now I am giving you a new commandment:
Love each other. Just as I have loved you,
you should love each other."

JOHN 13:34

How many different ways are there to love other people? That's a pretty impossible question to answer! There are probably as many ways as there are people! Certainly, there is no one way to love another; to limit ways we can show love would be to limit God, who IS love!

His commandment is to love people. We are not given specific instructions; all we need to do is love. There are, we know, ways to pervert love, but with God's leading, we can know where or how He is prompting us to love. It might be in a conventional way, like writing a love letter to our spouse, or it could be rather unconventional, like picking up a neighbor's runaway garbage can or telling your friend, with care and affection, your honest concerns about her dangerous life choices. Whatever the circumstance, love is possible, and we are the ones who get to pour it forth onto others!

November 11

A PLACE TO LISTEN

*I cried out to the LORD in my great trouble,
and He answered me. I called to You from the
land of the dead, and LORD, You heard me!*

JONAH 2:2

The "land of the dead" sounds like a pretty hopeless place, devoid, even, of life. There is no community here; there is no chaos, no noise, and no real uproar. There is just us, feeling nearly silenced by hopelessness and without another person there to revive us back to hopefulness. Where have you experienced the "land of the dead" in your life?

The thing about this land, which feels so barren, is that we are without an abundance of the distractions that may normally keep us from reaching to God. When our options feel so few, the one that we really should take is more pronounced. In a land that does not hold much life, our small voice sounds very loud. He, of course, can always hear it – but maybe it is in this desolate place that we will better be able to hear Him calling back to us.

In the midst of loneliness and despair, listen! You're not alone!

WITH US

The LORD will not abandon His people, because that would dishonor His great name. For it has pleased the LORD to make you His very own people.

1 SAMUEL 12:22

It's a tough thing to swallow when a president prematurely steps down from serving the people, a coach quits leading her team, or a boss walks away from her employees. These things happen, but it's not without questions, conflict or pain. It's simply not natural for us to abandon the people we are leading and serving.

God, however, will not abandon us. We are not simply a job to Him; He not only created us, but He first imagined us. He dreamed us up and then shaped us into being. He created this entire earth to run around, play in, cultivate and care for. He is Immanuel, God with us – so He will not be without us! To do so would go against the very nature of who God is and what His purpose is for creation.

We may often feel the very real fear of abandonment, but in Immanuel, we are joined eternally.

November 13

NOTICING THE GLORY

If you are suffering in a manner that pleases
God, keep on doing what is right, and trust your lives
to the God who created you, for He will never fail you.

1 PETER 4:19

What sort of pain have you endured that you could, at the same time, rejoice in? That sounds a bit illogical, but consider childbirth, for example. There is not much in the realm of physical pain that matches the pain of labor. And yet, what glorious affliction for, at the end of it, you hold your newborn child, her body against yours, and it all is worthwhile.

Living for God in this world will not come without hardship. We may have to go against the flow, defend our faith, and come by ridicule. And yet, what glorious affliction – all of our difficulties on earth will be soon forgotten when we're painlessly celebrating in heaven for all of eternity.

What afflictions are burdening you today? Can you keep your eye on the glory to come from the pain?

November 14

5 MINUTES WELL SPENT

*"If you are even angry with someone, you are subject
to judgment! If you call someone an idiot, you are in
danger of being brought before the court. And if you
curse someone, you are in danger of the fires of hell!"*

MATTHEW 5:22

Eating a cupcake is not a bad thing. But things spin a bit out of control when we eat another, and then another, and then another. Before we know it, our entire dinner consisted of nothing but cupcakes. What started off as a delicious treat, soon spiraled into something gluttonous and unhealthy.

The emotion of anger can be a gateway to regrettable actions. Anger can lead us to speak and act with abandon. Anger leaves us in danger of behaving wrongly, in ways that are dishonoring to everyone involved (ourselves, the other person, and God). We will feel anger. It is a human emotion – but it's what we do with the anger that matters so significantly. What if we took a pause before moving forward with our passionate (and sometimes very valid) anger? What sort of calming refocus could we get from even 5 minutes of centering ourselves? Consider it worthwhile!

November 15

LEVEL GROUND

*I will thank the LORD because He is just; I will
sing praise to the name of the LORD Most High.*

PSALM 7:17

Imagine getting in trouble for a wrong that both you
and your best friend committed, except you are the
only one who was punished! How unfair is that? If
the scenario was different, however, and we got off
scot-free while our best friend was subjected to a
rather harsh punishment, that really wouldn't feel
very good, either, would it?

If we're being honest, we all desire to live in a just
society. When laws within our country or world are
unfair, it feels pretty outrageous. But, when justice
reigns, everybody has a fair chance (and, really, isn't
that how it should be?). In impartial societies, we are
all subjected to the same standards – following the
rules put into place for our environment.

Our God is a God who is all about justice. He
gives everyone a chance, and no amount of money,
fame, or right motives can make us exempt from His
punishment or pleasure.

November 16

REVEALING OUR STAINS

People who conceal their sins will
not prosper, but if they confess and
turn from them, they will receive mercy.

PROVERBS 28:13

It is so disappointing (and slightly embarrassing!) when we have a stain in the middle of our carpet. Scrub as we may, it simply will not fade. So, what do we do? We, of course, find an attractive rug to put over the bold discoloration. We make it look like the rug is meant to be there, like it's all a part of the room's design!

No matter how nice the rug looks, the truth is, we know what's under it. Likewise, our sins will not disappear with a covert cover-up. We know that they exist, and try as we might to ignore them, we cannot escape the truth of their existence. If we were to admit their presence, then maybe we could move along without being fearful that someone will uncover our sin. Or, through Christ's sacrifice, we can confess and repent, and our sins are wiped away (like a holy stain remover!).

Lift the rug – experience mercy!

November 17

SUBJECTIVE SCORING

As for me, it matters very little how I might be evaluated by you or by any human authority. I don't even trust my own judgment on this point. My conscience is clear, but that doesn't prove I'm right. It is the Lord Himself who will examine me and decide.

1 CORINTHIANS 4:3-4

The sport of gymnastics is both beautiful and exciting to watch; the athletes perform so skillfully and courageously. What is often frustrating, however, is that gymnasts are scored subjectively. Their routine may be outstanding in the eyes of one judge, but riddled with minor technical deductions in another judge's opinion. We know, too, that outside factors can sometimes subconsciously affect scoring. A judge may be exhausted, ill, or enduring difficult personal trials. Because of this, we cannot ever really know the true score of a gymnast's routine, because it is based on the informed opinion of each individual judge.

Our judgment of others is also subjective. We may have sound advice and helpful thoughts to offer someone, but we know that God is the one who will have the final, most loving and fair judgment. We can leave the judging to Him!

November 18

DISINTEREST IN "HOW"

Don't worry about anything; instead, pray about
everything. Tell God what you need, and thank Him for
all He has done. Then you will experience God's peace,
which exceeds anything we can understand. His peace
will guard your hearts and minds as you live in Christ Jesus.

PHILIPPIANS 4:6-7

Think of all the things you use on a daily basis that work faithfully, though you cannot explain how they work. And, to be honest, you don't really need to know! When you send an email, for example, are you aware of the details of all that is happening in cyberspace in order to get that email delivered to the recipient? It's sort of mind-boggling! Most of us, however, aren't concerned with how it works – we just know that it does!

The peace of God is beyond comprehension. It is not only a peace that we cannot wrap our heads around, but we simply don't feel the need to try to figure it out. All we know is that we can trust Him – with our anxiety, fear and uncertainties – and we don't have to exhaust ourselves in wondering how everything will work out, we just believe it will! That kind of peace gives us room to enjoy life!

November 19

LOVE, BY EXTENSION

Everyone who believes that Jesus is the Christ
has become a child of God. And everyone
who loves the Father loves His children, too.

1 JOHN 5:1

Has your sister (or best friend) ever given birth? What an incredible event! This woman, who you love so dearly and know so deeply, has brought a little human into the world! Although you are not the mother, you will play a significant role in this child's life, as someone who is so closely connected to his mother. There may be moments when you grow irritated with this child, but you will love it as truly and genuinely as if he were your own!

Our love for Christ leads us to love for His children. We cannot simply love God and then draw the line there, feeling no pull towards His children (just as we could not really love our sister without feeling love for her offspring).

We will get irritated with God's people (and we will irritate them, too!), but our love for Him should be such that it extends to His children.

November 20

FOREVER UPHELD

Don't be afraid, for I am with you.
Don't be discouraged, for I am your God.
I will strengthen you and help you. I will
hold you up with My victorious right hand.

ISAIAH 41:10

Sometimes, we need an advocate – someone who will speak out on our behalf (either to others, or to us). We need someone who will remind us of times we've exhibited strength; someone who can remind us of what we have done and can do in overcoming struggles. We need truth spoken into our lives. We need to be defended, encouraged, held and stood by.

When someone holds us up, they are essentially saying, "*You are worth being held. You are not too far gone or too heavy for me!*" We need people in our lives who can do this and we need to be people who will do this for others. And, above all, we need to recognize that our God is here, desiring to remind, hold and encourage us of these things. He'll hold us until we don't need to be held – and, even then, He'll stand by in case we need a boost every now and again.

November 21

SAFETY IN OUR LIMITATIONS

*People who long to be rich fall into temptation
and are trapped by many foolish and harmful
desires that plunge them into ruin and destruction.*

1 TIMOTHY 6:9

Where, in life, do you feel limited because of financial restrictions? What particular things does your budget keep you from doing? Do you wonder about the places you would go or things you would do if money were not an issue? Life would certainly look different in that case. While, for many of us, money may easily become a source of stress, our limited funds may actually be protecting us from harm.

Imagine how easy it might be to lose control with an abundant income. We would have to work even harder to hold on to our boundaries and values. What if, with lots of money, we are slowly plunged forward into a life where the money leads us? It could lead us to various countries and fancy social gatherings, but it would also be leading (or dictating) our morals and values.

An endless income may sound gratifying, but our safety may be in our limitations!

GIVE AND RECEIVE

*"Do to others whatever you
would like them to do to you."*

MATTHEW 7:12

Driving someone to the airport before dawn is miserable. We don't have the excitement of traveling, and we don't have time to go back to sleep when we get home! Sometimes, however, we will need to be driven to the airport before the sun rises and, when we do, we hope that someone will make that early-morning drive for us!

So we keep this in mind when our friends ask for a 4AM ride. We get in the car and we drive them, because we would want them to do it for us.

If we are treating others with the love and respect we want to receive, then it may not only be easier for them to offer it back to us, but we'll be setting a tone in the relationship – one of genuine love and kindness.

When we offer kindness to others, we can't lose – we're enriching their lives and maybe they, too, will then enrich ours!

November 23

BOLD LOVE

*"This is how God loved the world: He gave
His one and only Son, so that everyone who
believes in Him will not perish but have eternal life."*

JOHN 3:16

What is the boldest way you have ever communicated your love for someone? Did you quit your job, leave your hometown, or risk your pride in order to show this person how you felt? Consider the sacrifice that this confession of love required of you. It is pretty difficult to show someone we love him without sacrificing something. Love is selfless, which leads us to want to sacrifice for another.

Jesus died on the cross because God loves us so deeply. God did not send His Son simply to show the world what sacrifice looks like; He did it because of love. There was no other way that God could communicate the depth of His love to us, than to sacrifice so severely. That was done for us!

He needs you, specifically, to know the gravity of His sacrifice, because it was done out of love for you. What bold and selfless love!

November 24

WHEN THE CAT'S AWAY, THE MICE WILL WORK

Work willingly at whatever you do, as though you were working for the Lord rather than for people.

COLOSSIANS 3:23

What's it like when the boss goes out of town? Does the office remain as productive as it usually is? Do you find yourself checking your personal email or social media accounts a bit more frequently with your supervisor not around to look over your shoulder at any moment? Maybe you waltz in a few minutes late or leave slightly early for the day because, let's be honest, your boss will never know!

Living with integrity leads us to live more godly lives, no matter who is watching us. Whether our boss is looking over our shoulder or not, we will do well the job we were hired to do, because that is the right thing to do. When we slack off just because our boss is gone, we're communicating that we're only working to please our boss, with no regard for our own character or position.

May our integrity remain, even if our boss is gone!

November 25

CROOKED HAIR AND CROOKED LIVES

Look at the proud! They trust in
themselves, and their lives are crooked. But
the righteous will live by their faithfulness to God.

HABAKKUK 2:4

Have you ever cut your own hair? Women with particularly long hair may find this to be incredibly difficult. How do you cut the back of your hair in a straight line and/or without cutting into your neck? Most of us would not even try to give ourselves a hair cut because we're relatively certain it would be a recipe for disaster! We know better than to trust ourselves with something like that!

When we try to go about life trusting in our own self, abilities, and beliefs, then we're going to find that we make some pretty uneven or inconsistent decisions (and often cause ourselves more pain than necessary). Putting our faith in God and being able to let others in enough to trust their support, wisdom and skillset will help to keep us on a path that is less dependent on us and wholly dependent on God.

TURNING IN PRIDE FOR STRENGTH

I take pleasure in my weaknesses, and in the insults,
hardships, persecutions, and troubles that I suffer
for Christ. For when I am weak, then I am strong.

2 CORINTHIANS 12:10

What happens to our pride when we have to admit that we need help? Well, what happens is, our pride is disregarded because the help we need outweighs the pride we need – and it's worthwhile. Consider what we are inviting when we put aside our pride and ask for assistance. We are reaping benefits from a strength we didn't have on our own! So when our friend hears that we are too sick to make dinner or do the laundry, she steps in to do these things for us – not only do we experience her care for us, but we get food and clean clothes!

When we surrender our pride and ask God for help, He joins us in our life. In doing so, we are given boundless amounts of strength because we are working out of His, not ours. When we admit we need God, we receive His divine strength – what could be greater than that?

November 27

SPECIAL ORDER!

You made all the delicate, inner parts of my body and
knit me together in my mother's womb. Thank You for
making me so wonderfully complex! Your workmanship
is marvelous – how well I know it. You watched me as
I was being formed in utter seclusion, as I was woven
together in the dark of the womb. You saw me before I
was born. Every day of my life was recorded in Your book.
Every moment was laid out before a single day had passed.

PSALM 139:13-16

Can you believe that you are treasured enough to have been knit together uniquely and personally? We are not mass-produced – we are complex beings, each nose, toe and small intestine is hand designed!

No being knows our complexities or details more deeply and fully than God. He not only knows them, but He chose them.

You didn't accidentally slip passed Him when you were being formed and, instead, receive the craftsmanship of a rookie. You were hand-shaped by God!

November 28

BE SPONTANEOUS

"Sell all your possessions and give the money to the poor, and you will have treasure in heaven. Then come, follow Me."

LUKE 18:22

What is the craziest thing you have ever done? Studied abroad in an unexpected location, moved across the country "just because," or entered your first art show at a moment's notice? It can be fun to do some bold and unexpected things every once in a while – sometimes we can even surprise ourselves with our sense of adventure!

Living a life for God requires boldness, too! Life with Him is anything but boring. In fact, He asks us to embrace the wildness and spontaneity of the journey with Him; we may soon find ourselves selling our belongings, moving across the world, or writing a book. The fun part is that we don't really know all of the adventure that is in store for us when we commit to living for God, but we can trust that He will be with us – and that our sacrifices will be returned to us, in excess, when we enter heaven!

Mallory Larsen

BETTER THAN A COUPON!

*The wages of sin is death, but the great gift
of God is eternal life through Christ Jesus our Lord.*

ROMANS 6:23

You're out shopping for clothes, on a tight budget but with a coupon in hand, at your favorite store! You soon find the perfect outfit but, as the cashier is ringing it up, he looks up at you with regret: "I'm sorry," he says, "your coupon is not valid for this article of clothing." This is the worst news!

"But," he continues, "you're here on the right day. We're having a 75% off sale for everything in the store. You'll get this outfit for even cheaper than you would have with the coupon!" This is the best news!

Our sin is costly, but God swoops in and offers us a deal better than we could have imagined! We would be subjected to death, but Jesus came to earth, sacrificing His life, and now we're offered eternal life! We didn't even have to show up on the right day to receive life; the gift is always ours for the taking!

November 30

December

WHAT'S NEXT AND WHAT'S NOW

We long for our bodies to be released from sin and suffering. We, too, wait with eager hope for the day when God will give us our full rights as His adopted children, including the new bodies He has promised us.

ROMANS 8:23

"Are we there yet?" What happens when we're constantly asking this while on a road trip? Well, besides irritating those we are with, what happens is – nothing! We're not arriving at our destination any faster and we're missing the journey because we're so focused on when it will end!

As Christians, we have much to look forward to. But if we're so focused on what we'll gain in heaven, we're going to miss out on the riches God has prepared throughout the journey for us here, in our lives on earth. The anticipation of what's to come is so very sweet, but it should not pull us away from being present for the ride we're on now. What are you most looking forward to about the anticipation of heaven? Now, what are you most enjoying about your life now? Let's allow both to co-exist!

December 1

YOUR LEGACY

*Those who are wise will shine as bright
as the sky, and those who lead many to
righteousness will shine like the stars forever.*

DANIEL 12:3

Regardless of how much time we spend on this earth, we create a legacy for ourselves. Some will be positive, others negative. Some of us will have a worldly-focused legacy, others will be God-centered. If you were to die today, what would others say about you? How would you be remembered? These are big questions and are not always easy to think about, but they may lead us to reconsider the way we are living our life, so that we can pursue a life lived with a godly impact on our world.

In addition, we do not have to have a world-renowned legacy in order for it to matter. To do good for others and to honor God – that is what creates an eternal legacy. Even if we impact only one life during our time on the earth – one life matters, and that would lead us to having a significant impact during our time in this world.

December 2

HOW IT IS VS. HOW IT SHOULD BE

Their disagreement was so sharp that they separated.

ACTS 15:39

Let's be honest: it is hard to work with people. Have you ever been assigned to a partner at work or in school and ended up despising them because of your differences in opinion? Disagreements will happen, but consider the cost when we let them be severe enough to where we lose relationship with others.

God gave us one another so that we can work together, expanding our ideas and supporting one another. That is, of course, easier said than done, but it is such a perversion of His desires for us when our differences with others separate us indefinitely. When that happens, we can almost hear the Spirit groan, "This is not how it's supposed to be!" There are some things about the way things are that we cannot change, but when we fight to keep relationships intact, we're doing our part to move the world more towards how things are supposed to be.

December 3

CARRYING SUNSHINE

I am disgusted with my life. Let me
complain freely. My bitter soul must complain.

JOB 10:1

Have you ever seen a cartoon where a rain cloud follows around just one of the characters the entire time, while the rest of the world is sunny? Not only does that character look miserable, but nobody else is particularly excited he's around, either. He's ruining the sunny view with his dark rain cloud!

It's not hard for our complaints to dominate our dialogue and, before we know it, we're carrying around a figurative rain cloud. Not all of life is sunshine, of course, but we have hope, so our complaints should carry less weight. Let's focus on a Kingdom perspective, recognizing that our difficulties and discomforts are valid, but we are here for only but a while, and then we are ushered into a place of perfection and glory.

Misery on earth may not get us to heaven any faster, and it's dampening the experience of everyone around us!

December 4

Mallory Larsen

SIN LEADING TO REPENTANCE

They have no sense of shame. They live for lustful pleasure and eagerly practice every kind of impurity.

EPHESIANS 4:19

What happens when you get caught doing something you shouldn't be doing? Does your heart beat fast and your cheeks get hot? Do you want to run and hide in shame, or immediately start trying to explain yourself? Maybe you stand still, unsure of what to do or say; or you stand still feeling, really, nothing at all.

We know that we will all sin – that is no secret. But what we do in response to our sin is an important factor. When we commit wrongdoings, do we feel remorseful or emotion-less? Instead of feeling bad and so continuing to do bad, God wants to see our negative behavior spur us toward wanting to do good. If repentance plays no role in our sin, then we will only fall deeper into sin.

Shame may come with our missteps but, in our shame, we can pursue repentance!

December 5

PAYBACK TIME

Give to everyone what you owe them.

ROMANS 13:7

"I'll pay you back, I promise!" When you hear those words, do you ever just nod and smile, knowing full well that you'll never be seeing that repayment? Although it's not a tragedy, it is frustrating when our loan is forgotten. It feels dishonoring to us, and our agreement.

There are acts of kindness and generosity that need no repayment, but we should all be upright in returning to others what we owe to them, be it money, an outfit or a lawnmower. This is a very practical element of living a godly life; character and integrity are required in committing to loan repayments. What if we are almost certain that the lender forgot about our debt; do we still have to pay it? We all know the answer to that!

If the lender forgives it, celebrate; if the lender receives the repayment, be grateful for their generosity in the first place!

December 6

RIGHTING WRONGS

*Meanwhile, Zacchaeus stood before the
Lord and said, "I will give half my wealth to
the poor, Lord, and if I have cheated people on
their taxes, I will give them back four times as much!"*

LUKE 19:8

What, from your past, follows you? Is there a situation you didn't handle well or a way you caused another deep pain that has left you with a guilt-ridden memory you cannot escape? Those can be painful recollections to bear, but we are the ones who have the power to release ourselves from the hold those guilt-laden thoughts have on us.

It is never too late to right a wrong from our past, and the more we live in line with God's desires, the more we may feel prone to do so. Our mistakes do not define us and grace is so very real, but if we're feeling a tap on the shoulder from a past wrongdoing, it's a tap worth paying attention to.

What wrong needs to be made right in your life? God will delight in our attempts to rectify a situation, no matter how long ago it occurred!

December 7

PROMISES ARE
MEANT TO BE KEPT

Don't trap yourself by making a rash
promise to God and only later counting the cost.

PROVERBS 20:25

"God, if you help me to get this job, I promise that I will attend church and tithe every week; I'll volunteer at the food bank on weekends and I'll go to the dentist regularly!"

What sort of bargaining skills do we enact when we really want something? What happens if we end up getting that job? Will we even remember the promises we made to God in the midst of our anxiety and desire?

Making a promise is no small act, nor do we want it to be. If we're comfortable with promises being thoughtlessly made, then that does not give us much to stand on when it comes to God's promises for us. We hold tightly to vows He made to us, taking them on as our hope for this life.

How disappointing, then, that we would not offer Him promises with the same genuine intent.

December 8

TURNING BRAGGING INTO TESTIFYING

I have reason to be enthusiastic about all Christ Jesus has done through me in my service to God.

ROMANS 15:17

Imagine that someone contributed to medical research of a particular disease, for which researchers soon found a cure. What incredible news! What if, however, the contributor began taking the credit for the cure? Wouldn't that be a bit mind-boggling? Of course that person did not find the cure; they contributed funds, which helped researchers find it! Instead of wrongly bragging about finding the cure, the contributor could express joy in aiding an organization who discovered it!

When we boast about the good things we've done in our life, we're wrongly bragging without giving credit to the One who has done the real work through us. God uses us to serve, love and honor His people – it is because of Him that we can love like we do. We contribute to His work, but the glory goes to Him. Instead of expressing pride in our work, let's offer a testimony of the work He's done through us.

December 9

SEEING STARS

When troubles of any kind come your way,
consider it an opportunity for great joy.

JAMES 1:2

The city is not a place that is very conducive to star gazing. The city lights, along with the pollution, make it difficult to see anything in the night sky! Drive a few miles out into the country, however, and the sky lights up with stars!

When we're facing a difficult circumstance, the last thing on our mind is joy. It's hard to imagine that pain and joy can co-exist; and yet, our pain often holds pockets of joy – we just need the eyes to see them. Sometimes, when our circumstances feel the darkest is when we can see the areas of light and goodness (that may always be there). We can notice our supportive community surrounding us, and God upholding us with grace and strength. We can consider how we're being shaped through our difficulties, and we can anticipate the goodness to come from the pain we're in.

When the darkness feels overwhelming – look up and notice joy!

December 10

CREATING SPACE

Be humble and gentle. Be patient
with each other, making allowance for
each other's faults because of your love.

EPHESIANS 4:2

Does your spouse or loved one have irritating habits that have eventually become endearing to you? You no longer mind the way he bites his nails or chews the inside of his cheek. It's a part of him that you have grown fond of, even though it often used to drive you crazy! Love has a way of making room for our oddities!

Our tenderheartedness for others should make it possible for us to be patient and accepting of another person's mistakes. Although we, of course, should not grow endeared to sin, when we love other people, we have a greater capacity to accept (and forgive) their quirks and their failures.

Whether it's a bad habit or a hurtful sin, our gentleness and understanding communicates a love that has space for our humanness. We all need this sort of space because, after all, we're human.

December 11

BETTER THAN A SPA DAY

The LORD gives His people strength.
The LORD blesses them with peace.

PSALM 29:11

What do you need when you're going through a difficult time? Maybe you're not sure what you need, but you attempt to soften the pain with chocolate, a funny movie or a long nap. Your friends may come over with dinner and a hug. You might even treat yourself to a day at the spa. There are countless things we can do to try and get ourselves through hardships.

None of those are bad things. God, however, just might have the best offer for us. He can offer us strength to face our difficulties, so we are not simply attempting to run from them. In addition, He gives us peace to know that we will get through our hardship. His strength and peace should be at the core of our strategy for getting through difficult times.

There, too, may be chocolate, funny movies and spa days, but His strength and peace will be our guide in overcoming life's obstacles.

December 12

MORE IN STORE

I am with you, and I will protect you wherever you go.
One day I will bring you back to this land. I will not leave you
until I have finished giving you everything I have promised you.

GENESIS 28:15

How fun is it when we finish opening all of our birthday presents and then a friend steps forward and says, "Nope! You're not done yet! I have a gift for you, but you won't get it until next week!" How exciting! Our birthday celebration will last for another week! What a sweet surprise!

There is a lot in store for us in our life with God. We are still waiting to see what else God does through us in this life, as well as looking forward to Jesus' anticipated return and our move to heaven. Isn't it exciting to know that God is not done yet? He is still playing an active role in our world and He has told us that there are miracles and happenings still to come, but we just don't know of them yet.

That's a lot to look forward to! Do you feel His presence? He's here – leading us to more of His work!

December 13

GOING AGAINST THE FLOW

Pure and genuine religion in the
sight of God the Father means caring for
orphans and widows in their distress and
refusing to let the world corrupt you.

JAMES 1:27

Your friend comes over rather late and unexpectedly on a Saturday night. She is distraught, struggling in various areas of her life and feeling hopeless and depressed. She needs a friend, and she chose you. You, however, were on your way out the door. You do not just have plans tonight; you've been invited to an exclusive event downtown – a perk that may never come around again. Your friends are texting, asking where you are and urging you to tend to your friend tomorrow – tonight is for partying!

When we live our lives for God, rather than the world, we have to make some pretty unpopular decisions. Refusing to let the world corrupt us means that we live not by its standards, but by God's. We make decisions as He would (meaning we stay with our hurting friend, rather than go to the party), and we see others as He does. Popularity will not define us, but love will.

December 14

CLINGING TO GOD

*Don't love money; be satisfied with
what you have. For God has said, "I will
never fail you. I will never abandon you."*

HEBREWS 13:5

You are hosting a dinner party at your home for several people. After cooking all day, the time draws near for the guests to arrive. Suddenly, you are hit with the overwhelming fear that you have not prepared enough food. This is a disaster! But, why? There may not be enough food in the dishes specifically prepared for the meal, but there is a refrigerator and pantry full of food in the kitchen – no one will go hungry!

Many of us with "enough," are afraid of a day when we will not have enough. This fear leads us to put our money on a pedestal, since we are so anxious about losing it. What, though, are we so afraid of? What fear is relieved when we cling to our money?

God tells us that He will not fail us; maybe if we loosened the grip on our money, we could see how He will provide for us!

December 15

THE SECRET'S OUT!

Not that I was ever in need, for I have learned how to be content with whatever I have. I know how to live on almost nothing or with everything. I have learned the secret of living in every situation, whether it is with a full stomach or empty, with plenty or little. For I can do everything through Christ, who gives me strength.

PHILIPPIANS 4:11-13

If we're being honest, we're really all just trying to figure it out how to live life well. There are as many unique circumstances in this life as there are people – some of us are rich, some are poor, some are overwhelmed. Whatever the situation, the same is true for all of us – it's been figured out! What we need to do is put our trust in God. The not-so-secret secret to living is letting Christ live in us. When we do, we can thrive as His children, whether we're living in material abundance or scarcity.

Just because this is a "simple" not-so-secret secret, does not mean that it's easy! Contentment with our circumstance and the surrender of our own strength in order to receive God's strength requires humility and faith – and, yet, we can do it. How? Through Christ, who gives us strength. Imagine the possibilities when we're living life in His strength!

December 16

SOUL CLEANING

*Get rid of all bitterness, rage, anger, harsh words,
and slander, as well as all types of evil behavior.*

EPHESIANS 4:31

There is nothing quite as satisfying (or toiling) as spring cleaning. This is the sort of deep cleaning that we save for once or twice a year, when we're feeling particularly motivated (and tired of the layers of dust and piles of junk scattered throughout the house). When we take the time to do a deep clean, we often take stock of the things we're holding on to. What can we get rid of; what don't we need that is only taking up space?

It would serve us well to do some spring cleaning of our own character, heart and thoughts, too! Without realizing it, we can begin to collect jealousy, gossip, anger and greed within us.

If we commit to taking stock of the thoughts, emotions and behaviors we're holding onto, we'll be more prone to do some soul-cleaning – to flush away the behaviors that are only bringing discouragement and discontent into our life.

December 17

FILLING BALLOONS

Worry weighs a person down; an
encouraging word cheers a person up.

PROVERBS 12:25

We know that it does not take much to pop a balloon. With one poke of a pin, an inflated balloon can lose all of its air, falling helplessly to the ground. However, take a deflated balloon, either undamaged or well-repaired, and see how one pump of air will cause the balloon to begin to take shape. The more pumps of air received, the more fully the balloon will come into being, but one pump is all it takes to get the process started.

Even the slightest bit of anxiety or discouragement can be like a pin to a balloon, sending us spiraling into deflation. On the other hand, when we receive a thoughtful word of encouragement or act of kindness, it's a pump of air in our deflated balloon.

One kind word to another person may be all they need to get back on track – for their sense of self to begin taking shape once more.

December 18

SEARCHING (AND FINDING!)

Examine yourselves to see if your faith
is genuine. Test yourselves. Surely you
know that Jesus Christ is among you; if not,
you have failed the test of genuine faith.

2 CORINTHIANS 13:5

Do you ever spend your time doing one of those word searches published in a newspaper or magazine? Every word to find is listed next to the search; most of us never even question that those words are in the word search – we just have to use patience and focus in actually finding them!

To live in faith means that we believe God is all around us, even if we cannot see Him. Just as we trust that the words of a word search are there, to have faith is to trust that God is surrounding us, and we can even begin to notice Him. Do you see Him in bright sunsets, intricate flowers and sharp flashes of lightning?

Can you remember His presence as you look into the face of another, hear the sound of laughter or feel the rain falling on your skin? He is here, among us – we just have to notice Him!

December 19

MAKE ROOM FOR DIFFERENCE!

*Peter told them, "You know it is against our laws for
a Jewish man to enter a Gentile home like this or
to associate with you. But God has shown me that I
should no longer think of anyone as impure or unclean."*

ACTS 10:28

Much of our world's history is riddled with racism and discrimination. Much is to be grieved at the injustices that have occurred in our societies; injustices that continue to occur in various ways today. Consider the difficult question: how do you size someone up when you first see them? What do you notice about their race, ethnicity, body type, clothing, age or behavior? What conclusions are you quick to make based on what you see?

Racism and discrimination are simply not a part of God's kingdom. There is no room for that here; we are united souls, undivided by race, gender, and the like. God takes delight in the vast differences in His children – and we should, too! Each unique person comes with their own story, quirks and talents; when we write off people because they're different from us, we're missing out on experiencing the individuality they bring to our world!

December 20

LEAVING LAZINESS BEHIND

Laziness leads to a sagging roof;
idleness leads to a leaky house.

ECCLESIASTES 10:18

"I'll do it tomorrow!" is a phrase that is far too easy to say! We can be quick to put things off until tomorrow because our bed is so comfortable, our favorite movie is on or we just don't want to do it today. What, though, are we sacrificing when we choose laziness over productivity? In some scenarios, it may not seem like a big deal if we stay parked on the couch instead of honoring our to-do list; but, other times, our laziness could impact our quality of life.

Maybe our car needed new brakes or our smoke detectors needed new batteries – these are things that need to be in working order for the sake of our protection. What if doing it tomorrow is doing it too late?

Relaxing is healthy and necessary, but when a day of rest repeats itself consistently, we're in danger of living lazily, which is hardly living at all.

December 21

LIFE IN PROGRESS

I don't mean to say that I have already
achieved these things or that I have already
reached perfection. But I press on to possess that
perfection for which Christ Jesus first possessed me.

PHILIPPIANS 3:12

As a child, do you remember hearing a parent or teacher apologize for a mistake they had made?

What? You still mess up? But you're a grown-up!

Now, as adults, we think, *of course we still mess up!* We can often, even now, slip into thinking that the people we look up to have it "all together." Sure, we know that everyone is a sinner, but our teachers and leaders are pretty much done with that sinning stuff, right?

Wrong. We are all a work in progress – always! No matter how far along we are on our faith journey, we are still being molded as we learn about God (and ourselves). We can spend a lifetime discovering Him and still have only scratched the surface of who He is. We will not reach "completion" on this side of heaven, but we continually pursue it with hope, knowing that we will one day be whole with Him.

December 22

SAFE TO SPEAK

*You, O Lord, are a God of compassion
and mercy, slow to get angry and filled
with unfailing love and faithfulness.*

PSALM 86:15

Growing up, did you have a preference of which parent you would rather approach to confess a wrongdoing? Maybe you knew that one parent was a bit softer, patient or not so quick to jump on their emotions. Particularly when we are admitting places of failure in our lives, we'd obviously like to know we're being met with as much grace as possible!

God, who listens to us with compassion and acts purely out of justice, is safe to be honest with. What a relief to know that the One we are instructed to confess our sins to and ask for forgiveness from is full of grace and everlasting love.

Confessing our sins can be scary – and still may be, despite knowing God's character – but we should find encouragement and relief in knowing that His love for us will not waver, no matter our sin!

GROW UP!

When I was a child, I spoke and
thought and reasoned as a child. But
when I grew up, I put away childish things.

1 Corinthians 13:11

At what point in life did you have the realization that you are no longer a child? When you started your first job, moved to college or bought your first house? Maybe you're still having a hard time believing you're not a child anymore. The years often go by faster than we can realize and, soon, we're an age we always considered to be "old!"

Maturity happens – or, it should happen. We must allow for maturity to mold us and age us. Yes, we are always a work in progress, but by letting maturity imprint our behavior, we are encouraging the process of growth, giving it space to let it happen. We need to retire our whining, listen well to others and pay our bills.

Growing up is not always very glamorous, but maturity can cultivate our character in a way that reflects godliness. Embrace the new responsibilities and refinement that come with maturity!

December 24

SMALL CROWD, BIG MESSAGE

Even some men from your own group will rise
up and distort the truth in order to draw a following.

ACTS 20:30

What sorts of things have you done in order to get people to listen to or desire you? Maybe you've passionately led a protest or dyed your hair an off-the-wall color. We'll often hear of leaders or politicians running for office saying outrageous things in order to gain attention, or making promises they do not necessarily intend to keep. We all want to be well-liked and respected, but what lengths would you go to in order to draw a crowd?

The truth that we have to share with others is God's truth. Sharing anything other than that truth, whether to gain a following and be noticed or not, could be edging towards blasphemy. When we remain tied to sharing God's truth, we may not always draw huge crowds, but this truth needs to be shared. It is honorable work to speak out on behalf of God; we may not gain fame, but we will receive deep honor in heaven!

TELL IT LIKE IT IS

If we claim we have not sinned,
we are calling God a liar and showing
that His word has no place in our hearts.

1 JOHN 1:10

Has your name ever appeared on a public list you wish it weren't on – a list of people who haven't turned in their RSVP for a gathering, or who have ordered but not yet paid for their ticket to a group function. Maybe we even broke the law and find ourselves in the police blotter in our community newspaper. None of those feel good and, actually, can produce some shame within us. Yet, there is no denying the truth to the claims these lists make.

We are not perfect – none of us – and to declare otherwise not only contradicts God, but it sets ourselves up for contradiction. We are bound to fail (and that's okay) and, when we do, the jig will be up! Everyone will know we're not perfect (we already do).

We are not blameless, and though there is nothing to be proud of, we're all in the same boat – sinners saved by grace!

December 26

CHANGING OUR POSTURE

*They were calling out to each other,
"Holy, holy, holy is the LORD of Heaven's
Armies! The whole earth is filled with His glory!"*

ISAIAH 6:3

What sorts of things lead you to worship? When you see your baby open her eyes for the first time, you learn you're in remission, or you gather around the table with friends and laugh until tears stream down your face – are these moments that usher you into worshipping God? Or what about a sunny day, a night of uninterrupted sleep or a piece of chocolate cake? Life is full of good things, beautiful creation and answered prayers.

That, of course, is not all life is full of, but when we live our lives with a lean towards worship, we may soon have the eyes to see a whole lot more to worship God for. When do you feel awe or gratitude that simply stuns you?

Those moments call for worship; may we live our lives looking around, eyes open and ears listening, so that we can notice the calls to worship. Amen.

December 27

SEASONS OF THE HEART

A time to tear and a time to mend.
A time to be quiet and a time to speak.

ECCLESIASTES 3:7

Life is fluid; we are constantly moving through days, months and seasons. There are unspoken understandings about what we do, see, eat, wear and listen to as seasons change. Most of us never even have to think about what season we're in; we simply look around, feel the air, and notice what the stores are selling!

There are, however, other movements of life – ones that are less fluid or consistent. There are moments when we need a great deal of introspection, and moments when our life calls for great deals of celebration.

There are seasons when we may feel pulled to listen, and others when we're inclined to speak. What are you noticing about the season that your heart is in? You can't know by looking at a calendar what your heart needs but, lucky for us, our heart knows before our head. Let it speak!

December 28

REFOCUS

"That is why I tell you not to worry about
everyday life – whether you have enough food
and drink, or enough clothes to wear. Isn't life
more than food, and your body more than clothing?"

MATTHEW 6:25

Can you imagine going about your entire day un-showered, wearing dirty clothes, and picking at left-overs and calling it a meal? You are frantically running around a hospital, tending to your loved one. No longer do concerns about your appearance, matter to you. Your perspective has changed dramatically; instead of being concerned about worldly things, you're with a loved one as she fights for her life.

We all need to refocus our perspective every once in a while. To be in the world, and not of the world, is not always easy to do. Soon, we can find ourselves taking on the values of our society without realizing it, obsessing about the label on our posses-sions or the balance of our bank account.

These worries don't exist in a Kingdom per-spective; God has us taken care of.

CLEAN SLATES

Anyone who belongs to Christ has become a new person. The old life is gone; a new life has begun!

2 CORINTHIANS 5:17

Most of us love a new year. Out with the old, in with the new! However fun or terrible the previous year had been, we all get a bit of a new slate as the calendar year begins again. These can be deeply hopeful times. We do not completely forget about what the previous year held (or the ones before that), but we get a shot at making new, fulfilling memories. Anticipation and curiosity are piqued as the clock strikes midnight and a new year begins!

Even more exciting than that is the chance to begin anew with our life in Christ. When we commit our lives to Him, our sins are washed away – we have been redeemed! It's a clean slate; anticipation and curiosity are piqued as we wonder about what exciting, impactful and sensational things we will do with our Christ-filled life!

May the hope in a new start usher us in to living honorably!

December 30

KEEPING THE STORY ALIVE

*Each generation tells of
Your faithfulness to the next.*

ISAIAH 38:19

What stories does your family like to tell when they gather together? Do you remember that one awful Christmas together? Do you reminisce on the hilarity of that cross-country road trip, or laugh about that time when Dad fell headfirst into the pool? Stories are a gift, and they are so important to keep alive. The most important stories we can pass on, however, are the ones we tell about God's love.

Remember that time He answered your prayer in big ways, or healed your ailing friend? What about when He brought peace beyond comprehension during a painful season, or returned our generosity with a double blessing? These are stories worth remembering and telling. They not only enrich our faith, but they keep God's legacy alive and His presence real. Our stories of experiencing God are ours, yes, but they can also belong to those around us. Let others hear and know of His goodness – pass it on!

December 31

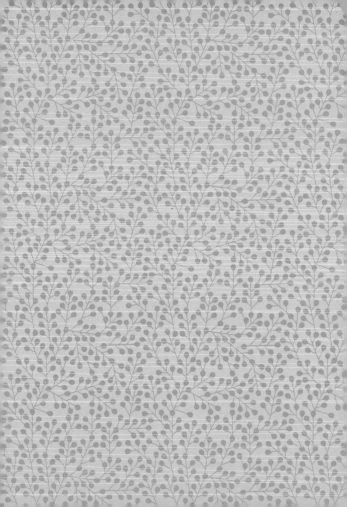

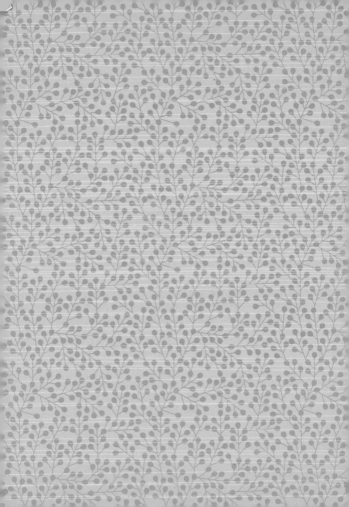